A HISTORY LOVER'S
GUIDE TO
FLORIDA

A HISTORY LOVER'S
GUIDE TO
FLORIDA

JAMES C. CLARK

THE
History
PRESS

Published by The History Press
Charleston, SC
www.historypress.com

Copyright © 2020 by James C. Clark
All rights reserved

Frontispiece courtesy of the Florida Department of Transportation.

All images courtesy of the State Archives in Tallahassee unless otherwise noted.

First published 2020

Manufactured in the United States

ISBN 9781467143387

Library of Congress Control Number: 2020940317

CONTENTS

ACKNOWLEDGEMENTS

For more than a decade, I have turned to Adam Watson at the State Archives in Tallahassee. The majority of the photographs in this book are from the archives. For this book, Jacqueline Attaway provided major assistance with gathering the photos. Rebecca Barber of the Florida Department of Transportation provided invaluable assistance in gathering the maps. My acquisitions editor, Joe Gartrell at The History Press, provided constant support with gentle good humor, as he has always done. I am also grateful to the University of Central Florida Faculty Center for Teaching and Learning for encouragement.

YOUR JOURNEY STARTS HERE

Former U.S. Senator Bob Graham calls it "Cincinnati Syndrome." It is the idea that people from Cincinnati move to Florida and live in the state for half a century but still call Cincinnati home.

More than any other state except Nevada, Florida is a state of transplants. One in four residents come from outside the United States, and more than one-third come from another state.

Back home, they may have taken Ohio history, Pennsylvania history or New York history, but they know little about the history of their new state. And even Florida natives learned U.S. history from the British point of view—the story begins at Jamestown or Plymouth Rock.

But the history of North America starts in Florida. More than half a century before the Pilgrims, Spanish explorer Hernando de Soto celebrated the first Thanksgiving in Florida. The first Christmas in what is now the United States was celebrated in Florida more than 450 years ago. Millions of Americans continue to follow a custom begun by the Spanish in St. Augustine, placing a single candle in a window at Christmas. Even St. Patrick's Day was first observed in Florida.

And on a darker side, the first cases of counterfeiting and insurance fraud were committed in Florida.

This book takes readers on a journey through Florida history. It is for those seeking to learn the basic history of the state and those who want to learn as much as possible. To be sure, it is an eclectic tour, with lots of side trips, but in the end, you will be an official Florida historian.

INTRODUCTION

The book starts with an overview of the state's history and then offers a huge bucket list of places to see. There are forts to see, along with state and national parks, museums and historic places. In all, you could spend years visiting the hundreds of places in this book. There are must-see movies involving Florida, a guide to major shipwrecks off the coast and a look at the major hurricanes.

There is a fort reached only by boat or plane, a hotel that plays host to the world's richest people, a hotel in St. Petersburg Beach where F. Scott Fitzgerald wrote *Tender Is the Night* and a bank in Ocala where Elvis Presley filmed a movie scene.

You will find out why George Washington didn't like Florida, what happened to Franklin Roosevelt's yacht and how Richard Nixon came to love the state. For those who want to know more, the book offers a guide to sixty books about Florida and a guide to finding out more in libraries and archives.

There are maps to help you plan your journey. They are arranged geographically so that no matter where you live, there are things to see just a few minutes or a few hours away. Think of this book as a user's guide to Florida and a tribute to the state's rich history. It is a veritable storehouse of information—some that shaped history and some that is trivial but fascinating.

Open to any page and start your journey through the place where the history of North America began.

5 FLAGS OVER FLORIDA

FRANCE

The French presence in Florida was brief, but it had great significance, leading to the Spanish conquest and reign of nearly 250 years.

In France, the Protestant Huguenots were persecuted and sought a place where they could practice their religion freely. They first established a colony in Brazil called France Antarctique in the mid-1550s. It lasted a dozen years before the Portuguese forced them out.

The Spanish tried to start a colony in Pensacola in 1559, but it ended in disaster, and for a time, the Spanish lost interest in Florida. The Huguenots were interested. In 1562, they made two landings, the first by Jean Ribault and the second by René de Laudonnière, who moved north and established a short-lived settlement in Parris Island, South Carolina. They encountered misery and internal discord, and the colony was abandoned.

Two years later, Laudonnière tried again, establishing Fort Caroline at what is now Jacksonville, but the Spanish attacked two years later and killed hundreds, although some did flee into the wilderness. Pedro Menéndez de Avilés even killed those who surrendered and hanged their bodies from trees with signs reading, "Not as Frenchmen but as Lutherans."

French soldiers who ended up at Matanzas Inlet as part of the plan to attack St. Augustine were slaughtered by the Spanish.

In 1568, Dominique de Gourgue joined forces with the Saturiwa Indians and attacked the Spanish at what had become Spanish Fort Caroline—renamed Fort San Mateo. The Spanish surrendered, but in revenge, De

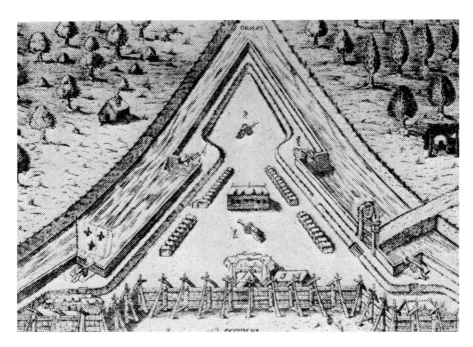

Above: The French built Fort Caroline near present-day Jacksonville to defend against the Spanish. The French lost the fort and their hold on Florida through military blunders and bad luck.

Right: Jean Ribault claimed Florida for the French, but the Spanish reacted and eliminated the French threat.

Gourgue slaughtered them and, as Menéndez had done, placed signs on their bodies reading, "Not as Spaniards but as murderers."

The French king thought little of De Gourgue's mission, and for several years, he was a political outcast before returning to active duty in the French navy.

In West Florida, the French had designs on the coast of the Gulf of Mexico. To stop France, Spain settled Pensacola a century after its first attempt ended in disaster. France established outposts in Mobile and Fort Toulouse, in what is now Mississippi. France and Spain resolved their differences and agreed to divide their Florida claims at the Perdido River, which is now the border between Florida and Alabama.

In 1763, France along with Spain was forced to give up its claims to the area after coming out on the losing end of the French and Indian War. Britain moved in, and that is when Florida was divided into East and West Florida, with capitals in St. Augustine and Pensacola.

France's efforts in Florida were over.

SPAIN

Spain found no gold in Florida, and those conquistadors who dreamed of great wealth found that not only were they not going to get rich in Florida, but also any conquest would be expensive. Florida was a money-losing proposition for the Spanish. They might have abandoned it, but two factors influenced their decision to establish settlements in Florida.

First was the interest of the French in Florida. Catholic Spain was tightly linked to the Vatican and would not permit French Protestants to settle the area and perhaps convert the Indians to Protestantism. Spain wanted to establish missions and convert the Indians to Catholicism.

The Spanish also found that the easiest route from the gold- and silver-rich lands in the New World back to Spain went along the east coast of Florida and then out into the Atlantic. Pirates knew the route and could wait for the Spanish ships to sail by. The Spanish needed an outpost to protect their fleets.

Juan Ponce de León came to the New World with Christopher Columbus on Columbus's second voyage and later became governor of Puerto Rico. He lost a power struggle with the son of Columbus and went in search of new lands. On April 2, 1513, he sighted land and named it Cape Canaveral. He then named what he thought was an island La Florida, for the feast of flowers.

The drawing may be overdramatized but shows the landing of Pedro Menéndez at St. Augustine in 1565.

No one can tell exactly where he landed—probably somewhere between Melbourne and St. Augustine—but we do know that his welcome was unfriendly and that three of his men were injured by Indians. There were three more landings as he headed south, as well as three more attacks by Indians. The Indians may have dealt with other Europeans who tried to enslave them. He planned to return soon and establish a permanent settlement, but his wife died, and he needed to care for his children. It was seven years before he returned, with two hundred settlers, animals and supplies. They landed at Port Charlotte, and again the Indians were waiting. Ponce de León was mortally wounded and taken back to Cuba, where he died.

More expeditions followed—Pánfilo de Narváez in 1528, Hernando de Soto in 1539, Luis Cáncer in 1549 and Tristán de Luna in 1559—but all failed. Spain seemed to be through, and even King Philip III said that Spain would make no further attempts to establish settlements.

Four years later, Philip reversed course and, under prodding from the pope, sent Pedro Menéndez de Avilés to remove the French and establish a Spanish settlement.

Florida became part of what was called New Spain, with land stretching from Venezuela to Florida. In Florida, Menéndez began building forts from St. Augustine to South Carolina and even sent soldiers to Cape Canaveral

After unsuccessful efforts, Pedro Menéndez finally established Spain's first permanent settlement in North America.

and Biscayne Bay. But Florida itself continued to be a financial loser, supported reluctantly by the other Spanish possessions and administered from Havana.

Menéndez also began building missions to convert the Indians. The Jesuits established missions along the west coast, but facing overwhelming odds, they turned the job over to the Franciscans, who established missions as far west as Tallahassee and north into Georgia.

As the British established their own colonies, they threatened the Spanish and launched several attacks on St. Augustine. St. Augustine remained firmly in Spanish hands, but the mission system began to shrink as the British colonies moved south.

The British pressure led Spain to ally with France in the French and Indian War. During the war, the British captured Havana, a far more valuable possession than Florida. The British offered Spain a deal: the Spanish could regain Havana if they gave up Florida.

With the British coming, the Spanish left, taking nearly all the Spanish residents and many of the slaves who had fled to Florida. Some of the escaped slaves stayed behind with Indian tribes. Spanish ships took them to Havana. Just eight Spaniards remained.

BRITAIN

When the British moved in, they found scores of empty houses and buildings in Pensacola and St. Augustine. The British broke Florida into two colonies, East Florida and West Florida, with capitals in St. Augustine and Pensacola, respectively. East Florida extended from the Apalachicola River to the Keys, while West Florida went from the Apalachicola River to the Mississippi and included Baton Rouge and Mobile.

The British were happy to have the Spanish out of Florida and to have eliminated a haven for escaping slaves, but just as the Spanish had learned, the British found that Florida was a financial drain. The British quickly encouraged trade with the northern colonies and Canada—something the Spanish had prohibited. Most importantly, Britain had no restrictions on bringing slaves into Florida and drew hundreds of plantation owners eager to find new fertile soil for their crops.

The French and Indian War created financial problems for the British government. The war was expensive, and afterward, the British government incurred more expenses supporting troops in North America from Indians and foreign enemies. King George III and his ministers thought that the colonists should bear part of the cost of their own protection and began instituting taxes.

As trouble brewed in the north, Floridians remained loyal to the king. They had no problems with taxes on items such as tea and wool and appreciated the presence of troops to protect them from nearby Indians.

Like Canada, Florida became a Tory outpost for those Loyalists escaping from the thirteen colonies and as a staging ground for British troops. For some Patriots, it also became a prison. Three signers of the Declaration of Independence—Thomas Heyward Jr., Arthur Middleton and Edward Rutledge—were held at the fort in St. Augustine.

Because of the escaping Tories, the population of St. Augustine soared and set off a building boom. The British surrender at Yorktown brought an even greater increase in Florida's population.

Spain had been on the losing side in the French and Indian War but this time was on the winning side, aligning with the French and the Americans. The Spanish helped by attacking the British fort at Pensacola, forcing Britain to keep significant numbers of troops in the city.

Now it was Britain's turn to leave Florida, although it took its time, thinking that the thirteen colonies might collapse and create an opening for the British to return. Spain would gain the territory as a spoil of war. This time, it was the British who sailed away to Canada, Jamaica, the Bahamas or England.

SPAIN

The Spanish who reclaimed Florida were not the same Spanish who ruled the New World in the 1500s and early 1600s. By 1783, their empire was under pressure everywhere, and Spain no longer had the power to administer Florida. For nearly forty years, Spain tried to rule an unruly territory as Indians, pirates, the American government and Florida residents tried their best to disrupt the Spanish—and often succeeded.

Spain had controlled land stretching from Florida to the Pacific Ocean, but Napoleon's sale of the Louisiana Purchase left Florida as an isolated, troublesome possession. The first blow came in 1810, when Americans attacked the Spanish at Baton Rouge, then part of Florida, and briefly established an independent republic. President James Monroe took the land and gave it to Louisiana.

On the other side of Florida, men from Georgia invaded to establish the Republic of East Florida but were turned back by the British fleet, which was increasingly aiding the Spanish. In the War of 1812, Spain again picked the wrong side, choosing to align with the British and opening Florida to British troops.

Andrew Jackson staged a raid into Florida, attacking Pensacola and forcing the British to leave. Jackson might have also driven the Spanish out, but British advances on New Orleans forced him to head west to defend the city.

Jackson was back in 1817 to put down trouble. He executed two British citizens he suspected of trading with the Indians, arrested two Spanish officials and established a government. President Monroe denied involvement in the plot, and support for Jackson's revolution collapsed.

The Spanish and the United States were growing weary of the Florida problem, and in 1819, Secretary of State John Quincy Adams opened talks with Spain, which led to an 1821 treaty giving Florida to the United States.

For the final time, and after nearly three hundred years since Ponce de León landed on La Florida, the Spanish left.

Andrew Jackson played a key role in Florida's early history, briefly serving as territorial governor.

UNITED STATES

No one thought that Florida would ever amount to much when it joined the United States in 1821. It had few people, little potential and plenty of problems. The Spanish were gone, and the United States finally had possession of a colony that had caused problems for decades. Andrew Jackson became the provisional governor but quit after a few months of uneven rule and returned to Tennessee.

The Americans kept the British system of East and West Florida and two capitals, in St. Augustine and Pensacola. The plan was to alternate legislative sessions between the two cities, but the travel between the cities was unbearable and the two sides agreed to meet halfway between, in Tallahassee.

Florida hoped to become two states—East and West Florida—and assumed that this would happen. It might well have, except for the issue of slavery. By the 1840s, when Florida became eligible for statehood, the South was trying to hold on to its power in the Senate by balancing the admission of free and slave states. Florida came in as a single state in 1845, paired with Iowa.

North Florida was attractive for plantation owners moving down from other southern states, while the rest of the state remained largely empty.

When the soldiers came to Florida, the government was forced to build forts in places such as Fort Myers, Fort Lauderdale, Fort Brooke (Tampa), Fort Gatlin (Orlando) and Fort Pierce. The troops needed roads and supplies, all provided by the government. To help attract people, the government offered free land near the forts, which drew settlers and changed forts into cities.

Meanwhile, the few hundred remaining Seminoles sought safety in the Everglades, and the army eventually ended the fighting, realizing that it could spend years and millions of dollars without tracking down the remaining Indians.

CONFEDERATE STATES OF AMERICA

Florida had only been a state for fifteen years when Abraham Lincoln was elected president. Florida was so opposed to Lincoln that his name was left off the ballot in November 1860. Lincoln promised not to disturb the institution of slavery, but few in the South were in a mood to listen.

Within days of the election, Floridians began to talk of secession. A convention was called, and the delegates voted overwhelmingly for secession. In January 1861, Florida became the third state to leave, following South Carolina and Mississippi.

Florida had the smallest population in the Confederacy with just 145,000 residents, and nearly half of those were slaves. While Florida could not send huge numbers of soldiers to fight, it became a supply depot for the fledgling nation. Florida produced salt—vital for curing beef and even making boots—along with cattle, which fed the Confederate soldiers. The state's extensive coastline was also attractive to blockade runners, who sought to avoid the Union-controlled ports along the coast.

Throughout the war, Union troops held Key West and Fort Pickens in Pensacola and, early in the war, took Jacksonville and St. Augustine. Florida had little military significance and was the site of just one major battle, an 1864 fight near Olustee. Lincoln hoped to capture Florida and return the state to the Union in time for the November election. The battle was a disaster for the Union, with troops routed and straggling back to Jacksonville. Tallahassee was the only Confederate capital east of the Mississippi not captured during the war.

When the war ended, Governor John Milton went to his home near Tallahassee and shot himself. Union troops moved into Tallahassee, and Reconstruction began.

UNITED STATES

Florida was in miserable shape at the end of the war. A third of the fifteen thousand soldiers who went to war never came home, and many of those who came home were missing limbs. The railroads were in ruins, the large plantations could not be maintained and no one was sure what would happen to the newly freed slaves.

Republicans took control of the government for a decade. Once back in power, the Democrats undid much of what the Republicans had done.

After the war, the tourists began returning, changing Florida's economy. The first visitors were sent for their health. Some thought that the Florida climate could cure tuberculosis and a long list of other ailments.

Harriet Beecher Stowe, the author of *Uncle Tom's Cabin*, moved to Jacksonville after the war, began writing about Florida's beauty and told readers how to buy land in Florida. Stowe's home on the St. Johns River became a tourist attraction itself, as steamboat passengers flocked to the railing of the ship for a glance of the best-selling author.

The Atlantic Coast Line Railroad hired poet Sidney Lanier to write about the wonders of Florida and distributed his writings to lure passengers. By the late 1880s, the number coming for health reasons had declined, but a new group of tourists were attracted by the railroads and hotels of Henry Flagler and Henry Plant.

Flagler, a cofounder of Standard Oil, first came to Florida as a tourist and then became a railroad and resort builder along Florida's east coast. Plant headed to Florida's west coast, building hotels and railroads. Flagler's landmark was the Hotel Ponce de Leon in St. Augustine, while Plant built the Tampa Bay Hotel. Both still stand and today belong to colleges.

The warm weather drew the wealthy and they came for "the season," stretching from December to March. The warm weather was the draw, but the tourists also wanted to see the sights. The state's first attraction was at Silver Springs near Ocala. Steamboats brought visitors to the clear waters. In the 1870s, the attraction added its famous glass-bottom boats to allow people to see the swarming fish.

In St. Augustine, Flagler's visitors were attracted to a spot displaying alligators that became Alligator Farm.

Flagler and his railroad moved south to Ormond Beach and then to Palm Beach, Miami and, finally, Key West. Plant started with a hotel in Sanford—the Pico Hotel, which still stands—and then expanded to Tampa. He built eight hotels and the state's first major golf course. Across the northern part of the state, William Chipley built his own railroad, dedicated to building industries, not drawing tourists.

With the coming of the automobile, tourism underwent a dramatic change. The Atlantic Highway (U.S. 1) linked Maine to Miami, and the Dixie Highway ran from the upper Midwest to Miami. Florida was within reach of two-thirds of the population. Carl Fisher developed Miami Beach and built a resort hotel, and by 1926, 2 million tourists per year were coming to Florida.

Visitors did not want to stay for just a few days—they wanted to own a piece of the state, build a home and enjoy life in the sun. Developers were quick to fill their needs, and hundreds of tracts of barren land took on exotic-sounding names to lure buyers.

In 1926, the boom turned into a bust as banks failed, foreclosures soared and the state got a preview of the Great Depression, still three years away.

By 1940, tourism had rebounded from the Great Depression, reaching 4 million visitors annually. World War II reduced the flow of tourists, but in their place came hundreds of thousands of soldiers who trained at bases from Key West to Pensacola. Many of those who trained in Florida made plans to return after the war or to retire to Florida. When the war started, Florida had the smallest population in the South. As the war ended, it became the fastest-growing state in the nation.

Three things aided the state's growth. First was the widespread commercial use of DDT at the end of World War II. It took years to learn of its harmful effects on nature, but while it lasted, it brought the swarming Florida mosquitoes under control. Second was the invention of the practical window air conditioner. Not only did it give relief from the summer heat, but it also allowed for an entirely new type of home: concrete block with a single air-conditioning unit sticking out. Before air conditioning, a concrete-block home would have been an oven, and homes required large windows for ventilation.

Social Security meant that older Americans no longer had to keep working until they couldn't do the job or to move in with relatives. They could sell a

After World War II, DDT was used to control mosquitoes in Florida. While it was effective, its use would eventually be banned because of damage to the environment.

Walt Disney and his mother had strong links to Florida. Walt Disney is best known for building Disney World, but his parents were married near Orlando.

home in the North, buy a cheaper home in Florida and count on a monthly Social Security check.

The end of the war signaled the start of the Space Age, and through a series of flukes, Florida played a leading role. The government planned to establish a missile launch site in New Mexico, but that proved to be too small. A second site in El Centro, California, was rejected because an errant missile might land in nearby Mexico. The Naval Air Station Banana River near Titusville was the default winner, and in July 1950, a rocket was launched from the Florida coast.

In 1958, the National Aeronautics and Space Administration (NASA) took control of the program that took men to the moon a decade later. The space program brought high-paying jobs and worldwide attention to Florida, but a decision in 1963 forever defined Florida. In 1963, Walt Disney was looking for a site for an East Coast version of Disneyland. He considered Palm Beach County, Niagara Falls and St. Louis before settling on Central Florida. On November 22, 1963, he flew over Orlando, saw the junction of Interstate 4 and the Florida Turnpike and said, "That's it." The swampy land he pointed to became Disney World.

Other attractions followed, including SeaWorld and Universal Studios, and Florida became the nation's number one tourist destination.

For Florida, it had been a remarkable journey from Ponce de León setting foot on Florida in 1513 to a journey to the moon in 1969.

10 EXPLORERS

JUAN PONCE DE LEÓN

Juan Ponce de León may have first seen the New World in 1493 on the second voyage of Christopher Columbus. His rise to power in the Spanish world was rapid, and within ten years, he was governor of eastern Hispaniola. He founded the first European settlement in Puerto Rico and became governor of the island. Rivals used their influence to have him removed, and as a consolation prize, he was encouraged to find new lands.

In 1513, he sailed along the coast of Florida, landing somewhere between St. Augustine and Melbourne Beach. He thought the new land was an island and called it La Florida because it was Easter and because of the lush vegetation he found. He sailed south around through the Keys and up the west coast to Charlotte Harbor, encountering unfriendly Indians everywhere he landed.

He became military governor of Florida and Bimini, but it was another seven years before he mounted an expedition to settle Florida. He landed near Charlotte Harbor with two hundred men and immediately encountered hostile Indians. He was wounded by an arrow and was taken back to Cuba, where he died. His original logs were lost long ago, and we have only a vague idea of where he landed along the Florida coast. There is a marker near Ponte Vedra Beach to mark the one spot we know where Ponce was the day before he landed. It is at the Guana Tolomato Matanzas Estuarine Research Reserve. There is also a historic marker on

Juan Ponce de León claimed Florida for Spain but was mortally wounded by Indians when he tried to establish a permanent settlement.

Duval Street in Key West to honor one of his discoveries, the Florida Keys. He had learned of the Keys from natives and claimed them for Spain. He named the Dry Tortugas for the huge turtles he found there and because there was no fresh water.

PEDRO MENÉNDEZ DE AVILÉS

In 1549, thirty-year-old Pedro Menéndez de Avilés patroled the Spanish coast for pirates, and five years later, he was named captain of the Indies fleet. Along the way, he made enemies and was imprisoned for years before he regained the favor of the king.

The presence of the French in Florida alarmed King Charles V, who sent Menéndez to establish a colony and drive the French out. With about two thousand men, Menéndez arrived in St. Augustine and built a crude fort. Within a month, he had captured the French fort to the north and massacred those inside the fort. He hanged their bodies from trees with the sign, "Not as Frenchmen but as Lutherans."

He helped establish forts as far north as present-day South Carolina before being recalled in 1567 to Spain, where he died. There is a marker on the grounds of the Prince of Peace Votive Church at 101 San Marco Avenue in St. Augustine to mark the Menéndez landing.

HERNANDO DE SOTO

Hernando de Soto was convinced that there was gold in Florida, and he went deep in debt to fund an expedition to find his fortune. He came to the New World as a teenager and soon was taking part in invasions in Central America. After conquering Nicaragua, he sought more adventure. He joined Francisco Pizarro in the conquest of the Incas and applied for a series of jobs before the king gave him permission to explore Florida. In 1539, he landed at present-day Tampa Bay with about six hundred men, along with horses, dogs and pigs.

He moved up the peninsula and then headed west. He spent the winter of 1539 in present-day Tallahassee and in the spring of 1540 set off into Georgia and the Carolinas. They turned west again and crossed the Appalachian Mountains into Tennessee. His mission to find gold or other wealth was a failure, and he turned south into what is today Alabama. When they arrived in the Indian village of Mobila (Mobile today), they fought the natives and then went west again, where he encountered another battle with the Indians.

He spent the winter in what is now Mississippi and then went to the Mississippi River; he and his men became the first Europeans to cross the Mississippi. In Arkansas, they failed in their search for gold and headed east

Hernando de Soto explored
throughout the southern United States.
He reached the Mississippi River,
where he died.

again. Back on the eastern side of the Mississippi River, De Soto came down
with a fever and died on May 21, 1542.

His men pushed on and eventually reached Mexico. For the many natives
they encountered, it was a visit from death. They contracted European
diseases such as smallpox that wiped out hundreds of thousands of Indians.
There is a historic marker in the De Soto National Memorial Park in
Bradenton at 8300 Desoto Memorial Highway.

JEAN RIBAULT

Had things worked out differently, Florida might have become French
territory. If that had happened, it would be because of Jean Ribault. In
1562, Ribault sailed from France with three ships and some 150 colonists.
The colonists were Protestants seeking religious freedom in the New World.
He landed near present-day Jacksonville and claimed the land for France.
He also sailed up the coast to present-day South Carolina. He established a
short-lived settlement in what is now South Carolina, then sailed for England,
where he was imprisoned, released and returned to the New World to aid a

Protestant settlement at Jacksonville. Ribault launched an effort to evict the Spanish from Florida, but a storm scattered his ships, and his flagship ended up on the shore south of St. Augustine. Ribault and the other survivors were executed by the Spanish. Ribault both started and ended the French effort at empire in Florida. There is a historic marker at the Timucuan Ecological & Historic Preserve at 12713 Fort Caroline Road in Jacksonville.

TRISTÁN DE LUNA

August 15, 1559, should be the day recognized as the start of the first settlement in North America. Instead, it is seen as the start of one of the most disastrous expeditions in history. When Tristán de Luna y Arellano sailed his eleven ships into what is now Pensacola Harbor, he thought he had planned for everything. There were men and women, soldiers and laborers, food and wine and military supplies. It was difficult to see how this expedition could fail. Other expeditions had fallen victim to lack of food or unfriendly natives, but De Luna seemed to have planned for everything. He decided to leave the supplies on the ship until warehouses were built.

The plan called for De Luna to settle Pensacola and then travel overland to establish a colony in what is now Parris Island, South Carolina.

A letter to the Spanish king claimed that "the port is so secure that no wind can do them any damage." Even before the king received the letter, the winds were blowing in the Caribbean.

Fifty men drowned when their ship sank—along with the supplies. Another ship took thirty-three crewmen to the bottom. Most of the colonists moved into present-day Alabama to await rescue. By the end of 1561, the colonists were gone.

De Luna was rescued by Ángel de Villafañe, who took him to Havana. He spent the rest of his life in Mexico, where he died in 1573. There is a historic marker at the Pensacola Visitor's Information Center at 1401 East Gregory Street near the spot where two of De Luna's ships were wrecked.

PÁNFILO DE NARVÁEZ

Pánfilo de Narváez was one of the Spanish conquistadors who played a central role in Spain's conquest of the New World. In 1526, King Charles V of Spain authorized him to conquer the lands from Florida to the west.

Almost immediately, Narváez ran into problems. He started with six hundred soldiers and colonists, but about a quarter deserted before the expedition began and another fifty drowned when two of his ships sank in a hurricane. When he finally left Cuba in 1528, he had four hundred men. He landed in Tampa Bay and started his expedition through Florida, encountering warring Indians and the swampy terrain. He and those who were left reached what became St. Marks after several months.

The original plan was for about 100 of his command to remain in Tampa Bay and then sail north to meet him. But his ships did not appear, and Narváez had his men build five ships of dubious quality. In September, the 245 survivors set sail along what is now the Alabama, Mississippi and Louisiana border.

The ships attempted to stay together but became separated, and the ship with Nárvaez on board was blown out to sea and never seen again. Of the four hundred men who sailed with him to Florida, just four survived. The four, led by Álvar Núñez Cabeza de Vaca, managed to reach Mexico after a six-year journey. There is a historic marker at Jungle Prada de Varvaez Park at Park Street and Elbow Lane in St. Petersburg to mark the spot where Narváez landed.

GIOVANNI DA VERRAZZANO

It is believed Giovanni da Verrazzano sailed along the Florida coast about a dozen years after Ponce de León. Verrazzano made his first journey to North America around 1508 and explored the area around Newfoundland.

As the Spanish increased their explorations, King Francis I of France knew that his nation had to launch explorations. He enlisted the Italian sailor Verrazzano to find a sea route to the Pacific. He reached present-day North Carolina in 1524 and thought that Pamlico Sound was the start of the Pacific Ocean. Sailing up the sound would surely lead them to China. His theory led to some confusion with mapping North America. He then headed north to what is today Canada. On a second voyage in 1527, he sailed to Brazil.

His third voyage, the one that involves Florida, is the most confusing. In 1528, he sailed for North America and explored the Florida coast and the Caribbean. His death is a mystery. It is thought that he landed at Guadeloupe, where the natives captured him, killed him and ate him, while his crew remained on their ships. There is also a theory that Verrazzano was the pirate Jean Fleury who was executed by the Spanish.

In 1527, Visconte Maggiolo drew a map of the North American coast from Canada to Florida based on the Verrazzano expeditions. The map is confusing to most observers because Canada is at the bottom of the map and Florida is at the top, but he clearly incorporates the Spanish designation of Tera Florida.

ÁNGEL DE VILLAFAÑE

Ángel de Villafañe is a forgotten Florida explorer despite his exploration of Florida, Guatemala and Mexico. He first came to the New World in 1523 and worked his way to become second in command to Hernán Cortés.

The Spanish had two problems in the Gulf of Mexico: pirates and storms. The Spanish ships sailing through the Gulf had little protection from either, and Spanish officials realized that they would need to establish a settlement on the Gulf Coast to protect treasure ships and more quickly respond to ships in distress.

The king of Spain sent Tristán de Luna to establish a permanent settlement on Pensacola Bay in 1559. The De Luna settlement was a disaster, facing a vicious hurricane, starvation and disease. Villafañe was sent to relieve De Luna and decided to all but abandon the colony. He left fifty men behind and sent the rest—about two hundred people—to Santa Elena near the South Carolina/Georgia border. Again, bad luck plagued the expedition. A hurricane struck his fleet, and Villafañe headed for Hispaniola and then to Havana. He spent several months in Cuba and then returned to Pensacola to pick up the last of the settlers and take them to Mexico.

Back in Mexico, Villafañe was asked about future colonization of Florida and recommended against it. He said that his advice applied to both the east coast of Florida and the Gulf Coast. Spain overruled his decision for a settlement on the east coast, deciding to establish a colony at St. Augustine a few years later. It was more than a century before there was an attempt to establish a colony on the Gulf Coast.

ÁLVARO MEXÍA

Forty years after the Spanish arrived in St. Augustine, they still knew little of the land and people to the south. They were establishing missions, but all to the north and west. In 1605, Spanish governor Pedro de Ibarra sent Álvaro

Mexía south on a mission to establish peaceful contact with the Indian tribes, primarily the Ais tribe.

Mexía traveled to Surruque (present-day New Smyrna Beach) and moved down to the aptly named Indian River. Not only did he make contact with the Indians, but he also drew detailed maps of the area and invited Ais leaders to meet the governor.

In September 1605, the Ais chief, known as Capitan Grande, came to St. Augustine with two other chiefs and twenty Indians. They negotiated a treaty calling for the Indians to return shipwrecked sailors to the Spanish and receive a reward. It was the first treaty with the Indians negotiated in North America.

ALFONSO FERNÁNDO GONZÁLEZ

Alfonso Fernándo González did his exploring nearly three centuries after the Spanish began exploring Florida, but his work was just as important and dangerous. In 1893, González—the son of the founder of the city of Fort Myers—and three other men left Fort Myers in two canoes provided by the Seminole Indians and headed east. They thought the trip would take four days, but it took two weeks; the four nearly died after running out of food and surviving on palmetto cabbage.

They moved up the Caloosahatchee River, through smaller lakes until they reached Lake Okeechobee, then through the Everglades. They abandoned their canoes and walked through the swampy terrain, barely covering a mile every two hours. They finally reached a railroad work camp, where they recovered. Their pioneering traced a route from the Gulf Coast to the Atlantic that would remain difficult for decades to come.

10 PIRATES

BLACK CAESAR

Black Caesar was one of the most unusual pirates to roam the seas off Florida. He was an African chieftain who evaded capture by the patrols seeking slaves to sell in the United States until he and twenty warriors were lured onto a slave ship by the promise of wealth and placed in irons after a fight.

The slave ship encountered rough weather as it neared the coast of Florida, perhaps brought on by an approaching hurricane, and as the ship sank, a friendly sailor released Caesar from his chains. Caesar and his friend boarded a lifeboat and headed to shore. They appeared to be the only survivors of the ship.

The two turned to piracy, posing as shipwrecked sailors in their small boat. When a ship came to their aid, the two produced guns and seized what they wanted. This went on for years, and they accumulated a fortune. Some believe that Caesar buried it on what is today Elliott Key, the northernmost key. He added to his crew, attacked ships and hid among the Keys when chased. In addition to gold and silver he stole, he kidnapped women and held them for ransom on remote islands. His headquarters was on a small island north of Key Largo, today called Caesar's Rock.

One of the strangest legends involves children captured by Caesar. The legend holds that some escaped and subsisted on berries and fish, formed their own language and became known as the "lost children."

In the early eighteenth century, he left Biscayne Bay and joined the pirate Blackbeard, and the two increased their raids on ships. Caesar and Blackbeard sailed on *Queen Anne's Revenge*.

In 1718, Blackbeard died in a fight with Lieutenant Robert Maynard on Ocracoke Island, North Carolina. Captured in the fighting, Caesar was taken to Williamsburg for his trial and execution. For modern treasure hunters, Caesar's favorite spot to make camp was south of Elliott Key in Biscayne National Park. The inlet is known as Caesar Creek, and the creek features a small island known as Black Caesar's Rock. If Black Caesar did bury his treasure there, no one has admitted finding it, although they have been looking for more than a century.

ROBERT SEARLE

The term *pirate* was open to definition. Some were murderous thieves out for plunder, while others were loyal to a single country and only struck at enemies of that nation. Some operated with the unwritten support of their home country, and others had even closer relationships. Robert Searle's early life is a mystery—even where he was born is in dispute.

By the 1660s, the situation in the Caribbean was confusing. Spain, which dominated the hemisphere in the 1500s, was gradually giving way to British power. British raiders attacked Spanish ships in the Caribbean, leading Spain to protest and demand restitution.

The British arrested Searle and held him in British Port Royal. The British were unsure what to do with him and, after a few months, released him to help with an attack of Spanish Panama City, Panama. The man who had been a British prisoner one day was a vital part of the British plan the next day.

In 1668, he captured two ships off the coast of Cuba and made plans to attack St. Augustine. He used one of the two captured ships as a cover, allowing it to sail into the harbor to a waiting crowd eager for supplies. As night fell, Searle and his men entered the harbor and moved ashore. A soldier saw them coming and sounded the alarm, but it was too late, as the pirates went on a murderous rampage, killing everyone they encountered. The townspeople awoke and fled.

Searle ordered an attack on the fort, but his guns could not penetrate its thick walls. He and his men gave up on their goal of taking the fort and turned to looting the town. The pirates killed sixty townspeople and stole the town's meager food supply. It was months before a supply ship arrived from Havana.

The attack by Searle convinced the Spanish that they needed to build a more substantial fort, and construction began on the massive Fort San Marcos. On the first weekend in March, there is a reenactment of Searle's raid on St. Augustine. You can join Searle's Buccaneers and take part in the raid. (You can find more information at hfm.club.)

DON PEDRO GIBERT

Don Pedro Gibert (or Gilbert) became known as the "Last of the Pirates." The South American pirate concentrated his efforts on South Florida.

Sometimes, pirates chased their prey or set a fire on the shore to signal distress and wait for a passing ship to fall into their trap. Gibert concentrated on an area that became St. Lucie Inlet on Hutchinson Island. He was so well known that a reef and sandbar in the area became known as Gilbert's Bar. He often hid out around the Indian River. Florida was a territory of the United States and lacked the naval presence needed to provide protection from Gibert.

In 1832, the American ship *Mexican* was captured off the coast of Florida by Gibert, who stole some $20,000 in silver. Gibert ordered his men to murder everyone on board and burn the ship. The pirates locked the crew and passengers in a room and set fire to the ship. After the pirates left, the men escaped the room and eventually reached land.

The British navy found Gibert and his crew on the coast of Africa capturing slaves and returned him to Boston for trial and an execution before a crowd of nearly twenty thousand. Gibert's era on the high seas was ending because of time and technology. As the U.S. Navy became stronger and forts were built along the Florida coast, steam-powered ships came into use.

Gibert's legacy includes a question about his treasure. Officials recovered some of the $20,000, but much was not found. The question remains: Did he bury some on the Florida coast? Gibert's legacy lives on around Hutchinson Island. There is Gibert's Pass (or Gibert's Shoal) and Gilbert's Bar—a sandbar off the coast between Fort Pierce and Stuart. The Elliott Museum features an eclectic collection centering on antique vehicles, but it also has exhibits ranging from baseball to foreign affairs. Gilbert's House of Refuge is still there, the last of a series of houses built to give sanctuary to sailors wrecked at sea. About one hundred yards offshore is the wreck of the *Georges Valentine*, an Italian ship that is a prime dive site.

SIR JOHN HAWKINS

To the English he was a hero, but to the Spanish John Hawkins was a pirate threatening their ships around Florida.

Technically, John Hawkins was a pirate. Although the Spanish despised him, the English and the French admired him. William Hawkins made his fortune by carrying slaves to the New World. His son, John, followed his father to the sea, with the blessings of Queen Elizabeth I, a Protestant who saw the Catholic Spanish as competition for the wealth of the New World. In 1565, the same year the Spanish settled St. Augustine, Hawkins was smuggling slaves to the Spanish when he sailed along the Florida coast.

He did not find the rich minerals he hoped for, but he did find Indians smoking pipes and bearing bodies with tattoos. The tattoos would take time to become popular among Europeans, but pipe smoking was an instant success. The British saw tobacco as the path to wealth in the New World. Near present-day Jacksonville, Hawkins helped the Protestant French who were facing ruin.

When Hawkins arrived, the French were starving due to a siege by the Indians. He rescued them and even offered to take them back to France, but they declined his offer and stayed to be massacred by the Spanish.

Hawkins showed there was wealth in the New World. To the French, he was a hero; to the British, he was a valued agent of the queen; but to the Spanish, he was a pirate. In 1595, he was part of an expedition that attacked Spanish Puerto Rico, but he died the night before the attack, which was unsuccessful.

FRANCIS DRAKE

To the British, Francis Drake was "The Admiral," but to the Spanish, he was "The Dragon." To the British he was a hero; to the Spanish, he was a wanton killer. His reign of terror in the New World began in Panama when he captured a Spanish ship loaded with thirty tons of silver. He was knighted by Queen Elizabeth I.

The Spanish called Francis Drake "The Dragon," who terrorized the Caribbean.

In 1585, he sailed with twenty-five ships and 2,300 men to attack the Spanish in North America. He struck at the present-day Dominican Republic and then at Colombia. His work done, he sailed back along the coast of Florida, where he and his men spotted St. Augustine. They marched to the town, where they faced a newly fortified Spanish fort but no Spanish soldiers. The soldiers and the residents had fled the city, leaving behind a small child in their rush to escape Drake.

Spanish snipers fired from the woods, but the English did not attack them, instead burning the fort and the town and seizing farming equipment.

Drake took part in a massive assault on Puerto Rico—the same one Hawkins was to participate in—but died of dysentery after the unsuccessful attack. The sacking of St. Augustine was captured in engravings by artist Baptista Boazio, who relied on eyewitness accounts (Drake may have provided the specifics) to show amazing detail about St Augustine. It is the first printed depiction of a European town in North America. A copy of the engraving is included in the map collection at the St. Augustine Historical Society's Oldest House.

ANDREW RANSON

In 1684, Andrew Ranson joined Captain Thomas Jingle in attacking the Spanish along the Florida coast. They captured a Spanish frigate in the Keys and sailed into the Gulf of Mexico, where they joined with five other pirate ships and prepared for an attack on St. Augustine. The attack on St. Augustine turned into a disaster. Storms blew five of the ships off course. Ranson pushed on, landing a party near St. Augustine to prepare to attack the town. Fifty Spanish soldiers surprised him and captured him. They used Ranson as a lure for the rest of the sailors on the bigger ships. Ranson waded out and signaled for the crew to come ashore. They suspected that something was wrong and fled, leaving Ranson and his men ashore.

Ranson was sentenced to be hanged, and his men were sentenced to hard labor. As the hour for his execution approached, he mounted the gallows as townspeople gathered around. The executioner twisted the rope around Ranson's neck until the pirate collapsed. Everyone assumed that Ranson was dead, but when a group of friars examined his body, they found he was still alive. The friars took his body to a nearby convent and pronounced his survival a miracle. The governor wanted the execution carried out, but the friars refused, despite the governor's insistence that a faulty rope, not a miracle, was responsible for Ranson's survival. A new governor spared Ranson's life.

Ranson claimed that he was an engineer and carpenter who could help with building San Marcos.

When the British attacked the fort, Ranson helped the Spanish. We don't know what became of Ranson, but he was the last pirate to try to capture St. Augustine. Some claim that Ranson is still seen in St. Augustine! According to local legend, his ghost haunts the fort, and supporters offer photographic "evidence" for proof. You can hear all about it on one of St. Augustine's ghost tours.

HENRY JENNINGS

Henry Jennings struck first in 1716 when he attacked the Spanish treasure fleet off the Florida coast. The Spanish had learned that the annual treasure fleet could survive by traveling in a convoy rather than single ships sailing alone. The pirates avoided the large fleet, with its great firepower. Some pirates followed the fleets, hoping to pick off a Spanish straggler or a ship blown off course.

The Spanish fleet left Cuba in 1715 loaded with wealth from Mexico and South America. Off the Florida coast, near present-day Fort Pierce, a storm wrecked ten of the eleven ships, sending the wealth to the bottom of the ocean. The survivors made it to shore and returned to Havana, where Spanish authorities salvaged as much of the wealth as possible. Indian divers recovered much of the treasure, which was stored on the shore. Ironically, Jennings was captain of an English ship assigned to hunt pirates.

Jennings abandoned his respectable life and returned to piracy. He learned of the Spanish salvage efforts and set off with three hundred men and five ships. The Spanish salvage effort was scattered, and Jennings seized 300,000 coins. Returning to Jamaica, he encountered another Spanish ship and captured it. He released the Spanish crew, but instead of fleeing, they followed Jennings back to Jamaica and saw the boisterous welcome he received.

After the first attack on the salvaged treasure, the Spanish did not increase security, and Jennings struck again two months later. The Spanish recovered most of their treasure and took it to Spain. Still, they left some on the bottom, and Jennings returned to launch his own salvage operation.

A new British governor in the Bahamas offered all British pirates a pardon if they gave up piracy, and Jennings quickly accepted, trading his life at sea for one of comfort and wealth. Near the site where Jennings and his crew made off with the 300,000 coins is the McLarty Treasure Museum, which is part of the Sebastian Inlet State Park near Vero Beach at 13180 North A1A on Orchid Island. The museum is centered on ships sunk in 1715.

JOSÉ GASPAR

It is ironic that Florida's most famous pirate never existed. Still, his legend has grown, and it is difficult to convince people that he is a myth.

The legend of José Gaspar begins with John Gomez, who claimed to have been a pirate. Gomez, whose own life is m'urky at best, sailed to the United States as a youth and said that he signed on as a crew member on a ship he claimed was captained by Gaspar. Gomez supposedly lived to be 122 years old, dying in 1900 while fishing near Fort Myers.

As for Gaspar, the story was that he was born in Spain and became a juvenile delinquent who kidnapped a young girl and was given a choice of going to jail or going to sea. He chose the sea. Or perhaps he was an

Even though there was no José Gaspar, he lives through the Gasparilla festivities in Tampa.

influential member of the royal court who fell out with the powerful and went to sea. Perhaps political enemies killed his wife and children? Supposedly, he captured some four hundred ships and settled on Gasparilla Island off the Florida coast.

According to the legend, Gaspar's end came when he spotted what he thought was a British merchant ship off the coast and gave chase. According to the legend, it was really an American warship that opened fire. Gaspar, worried that he would be captured, jumped overboard, shouting, "Gasparilla dies by his own hand, not the enemy's."

The problem is that while Gaspar was roaming the seas from the late 1700s until 1821, there were no contemporary accounts of his activities. Some assume that Gasparilla Island was named for him, but it was probably named for an early Spanish priest named Father Gaspar.

In reality, Tampa residents created the myth of José Gaspar around 1904. Eager to promote their city, they dressed as pirates and "captured" the city. The celebration grew over the years—a ship was added in 1911—and today has become a major event.

There are other legends associated with Gaspar. According to the myth, Captiva Island gained its name because it is the place Gaspar used to hold his female captives. The legend claims that Gaspar captured a beautiful woman named Joseffa and put her on a separate island. The island became known as Useppa, supposedly a mispronunciation of her name. José Gaspar might be a myth, but there is a Gasparilla Pirate Parade & Festival. It is held in Tampa in late January. (More information is available at gasparillapiratefest.com.)

LOUIS AURY

Over the decades, Florida has been a prime landing spot for smugglers. In the 1920s, it was illegal liquor brought from Cuba and Bimini to Florida's largely empty coast. In the 1970s, it became drugs, easily transported from Colombia or through a Caribbean island. But the smuggling began in the early 1800s, when the United States outlawed the importation of slaves. It was simple to bring slaves into the coastal area along the northern Gulf Coast. When the law became effective in 1808, Spain controlled Florida and was helpless to stop the influx. It was easy to transport the slaves from Florida to Alabama, Mississippi or Georgia. Even after the United States acquired Florida in 1821, the smuggling of slaves continued.

Amelia Island was a center for pirates and contraband goods, whether it was human beings or stolen merchandise. Louis Aury became a pirate after serving in the French navy. Angered when the United States seized his ship, he vowed revenge. He purchased a second ship, named it *Vengeance* and set out to attack ships from any nation. When that ship was burned while docked in Savannah, he acquired a third ship and signed on as a privateer for what is now Colombia. Later, he sailed under the Mexican flag when he captured Spanish ships.

Aury and Gregor MacGregor helped capture Amelia Island with a group of revolutionaries in 1817. He hoisted the Mexican flag and claimed that the island near present-day Jacksonville was part of Mexico. When MacGregor left Amelia Island, Aury took over, declaring martial

Louis Aury captured Amelia Island with dreams of setting up his own nation.

law. Aury even held elections to create a legislature and draft a constitution for what he named the "Republic of the Floridas."

President James Monroe grew tired of Aury and sent the navy to Amelia Island. The American flag was raised, and Aury was arrested and held for two months. His reign over Amelia Island lasted for three months. Congress passed tougher laws to regulate the slave trade and sent boats to patrol the coast.

Aury fled to Colombia to stage a revolution there but failed. He continued to attack the Spanish but met with failure. He never returned to Florida. But the pirates return to Amelia Island every year around May 1 when the Isle of Eight Flags Shrimp Festival is held. There is a parade featuring bands, decorated fishing boats, a giant shrimp and an invasion by the Fernandina Pirates Club.

WILLIAM BOWLES

Few people experienced as much as William Bowles, known as "Billy Bowlegs." He was born in Maryland in 1763 and ran away from home to join the British army during the American Revolution. While stationed at Pensacola, he grew tired of army restrictions and left to join the Lower Creek Indians, who made him a member of their tribe. He emerged as a leader and dreamed of organizing the Indians into an independent nation. The Spanish put a bounty on his head, and he turned to the British for help. The British wanted to support any plan to undermine the Spanish and gave Bowles a ship and supplies.

Back in Florida, he taught sailing to his Indian followers, and they attacked Spanish ships. He slipped only once, agreeing to a conference under a flag of truce, but the Spanish arrested him and sent him to prison—first in Cuba, then Spain and finally in the Philippines.

He escaped and made his way to Britain, where he received support and returned to Florida in 1799. He organized several Indian tribes into the State of Muskogee and went to war against Spain. His capital was a Seminole village near present-day Tallahassee. The new nation even had a flag and the slogan "God Save the State of Muskogee."

He attacked the Spanish fort at St. Augustine and, with his small army, captured it and held it for a month before the Spanish attacked and retook it. Bowles even formed a small navy and commissioned privateers to attack Spanish ships.

William Bowles deserted the British army to join the Lower Creek Indians. He failed in his attempt to organize his own nation and died in prison.

Bowles's undoing was the end of hostilities between Britain and Spain. The British no longer needed to support Bowles, and the Spanish could concentrate their efforts on tracking him down. The British even executed several of Bowles's privateers when they landed in what they thought would be the safe port of Nassau.

Spain offered a huge reward for Bowles, which encouraged some of his followers to capture him and hand him over to the Spanish, who moved him to a prison in Havana. He determined to die rather than spend his life in prison. He went on a hunger strike and died in 1805, his dreams of empire over. You can visit the birthplace of William Bowles and at the same time visit the town with the state's most unusual name: Two Egg, Florida. The origin of the name is disputed: some say it came about because poor families used eggs as barter, while others say someone once dropped two eggs and the name stuck. Two Egg is near Fort Walton Beach, which is the site of the Billy Bowlegs Festival. It is held the first weekend in June and features lots of boats, a parade and the landing of Billy Bowlegs and his pirate crew.

10 FORTS

FORT JEFFERSON

This is the most unusual fort in the United States, and just getting to it is a major undertaking. George Washington launched the United States on its first round of fort building, and by the time Florida became part of the United States, the nation was on its third round. Fort Jefferson—a fort that was never finished, was never used as a fort and would have been worthless in combat—was in the third round. Still, it earned a place in history.

It is the largest brick masonry structure in the United States with over 16 million bricks. In late 1824, Commodore David Porter came to the Dry Tortugas to find a site to build a fort to stop piracy in the Caribbean. He decided that the Keys would not do, but five years later, Commodore John Rodgers thought the Keys would be perfect. He suggested Garden Key, but construction did not begin until 1846. The fort was typical of the "Third System" designs launched after the War of 1812 to protect America's harbors. The fort covered sixteen acres, with six sides and three tiers of casements. The best known of the "Third System" forts is Fort Sumter in Charleston Harbor, where the Civil War began.

At the start of the Civil War, a small force of Union soldiers took Fort Sumter to prevent it from being taken by the Confederates, although its value was dubious. The problem with the fort was its brick masonry construction. From the time planning began until construction, firepower improved, and brick masonry was no longer the bulwark it had been. Fort

If you can get there, Fort Jefferson is the most remarkable fort in the United States. It is located at the tip of the Florida Keys and can be reached only by air or boat. It is well worth the trip.

Sumter is the best example of the drawbacks of brick masonry. Confederate cannons caused serious damage in 1861.

A failure as a fort, Fort Jefferson became a prison. Almost as soon as the war began, the Union used it for soldiers convicted by courts-martial and sentenced to hard labor. By 1863, there were 214 military convicts at the fort, and the number quickly increased to nearly 1,000 by the end of the war. The fort gained its fame in July 1865, when four men convicted of conspiracy in the assassination of President Lincoln arrived at the fort. Samuel Mudd, Edmund Spangler, Samuel Arnold and Michael O'Laughlen were found to have played roles in the assassination, although their roles were questionable. Mudd tried unsuccessfully to escape but was recaptured and placed in the fort's dungeon. He aroused the sympathy of the nation when yellow fever swept the fort, and he treated those who fell ill. The epidemic killed many of the prisoners, including O'Laughlen and the fort's doctor. Mudd, Arnold and Spangler were pardoned.

Yellow fever epidemics and hurricanes made it more trouble than it was worth. In 1889, the army turned the fort over to the Marine Hospital

Service for use as a quarantine station and the navy used it as a coaling station. It came to life again in 1898 when war with Spain broke out. The USS *Maine* used the fort to take on coal on its way to a fateful date in Havana. The fort was abandoned again and remained unused until 1935, when President Franklin Roosevelt designated it a national monument. Today, it is a national park.

Getting there is difficult. There is a daily ferry from Key West, and chartered seaplane service and a private yacht also provide service. Ferry visitors spend four hours on the island, which can include snorkeling on a reef.

Monroe County, Map 6; check it out at nps.gov/drto or call 305-242-7700.

FORT BARRANCAS

Fort Barrancas has been the site of a fort since 1698, when it was built by the Spanish, and today is within the Naval Air Station Pensacola. It began as Fort San Carlos de Austria, which was destroyed in 1719 when French forces captured Pensacola. When Britain took control of Florida in 1763, the Royal Navy Redoubt was built. During the American Revolution, the Spanish captured the city, and at the end of the Revolution, they retook all of Florida. By 1797, they had completed work on San Carlos de Barrancas (from the Spanish word for bluff).

During the War of 1812, the Americans joined with the Spanish and some Indian tribes to fight the British at the Battle of Pensacola in 1814. In 1818, American troops, looking for renegade Indians, attacked the fort and captured Pensacola. The United States purchased Florida from Spain in 1821, and Pensacola was chosen as the site for a large navy installation built around the original fort.

Between 1839 and 1844, the fort was rebuilt and enlarged to prevent ships from entering the harbor and given larger guns to fire farther out to sea.

Officials in Washington thought the Civil War might begin in Pensacola. Before the attack on Fort Sumter, Colonel William Henry Chase—who had built the fort before going over to the Confederates—demanded that Union troops surrender the fort. The Union troops fired shots at Chase and his Florida militia. The Union troops knew that Fort Pickens, located across the inlet to Pensacola Bay, would be easier to defend. Fort Barrancas was on the mainland and an easy target for the Confederates from Florida, Alabama and Mississippi. On October 9, 1861, Confederate troops tried to take Fort Pickens, but Union forces drove them back. There was a third fort involved, forming a triangle with Pickens and Barrancas. The next month, Confederate troops exchanged cannon fire with Pickens, and it appeared the battles might be the catalyst for war.

The attack on Fort Sumter in April touched off war instead. Almost as soon as the war began, Union troops captured New Orleans, and Confederate forces abandoned Pensacola.

Because of increased cannon firepower, Barrancas became useless, as did other brick forts built during that period. In 1947, it was deactivated and incorporated into the Naval Air Station. Fort Barrancas is part of the Gulf Islands National Seashore and is operated by the park service. It is open Thursday through Monday, and tours by the rangers can be arranged.

Escambia County, Map 3; for more information visit nps.gov/guis.

FORT MATANZAS

Fort San Marcos in St. Augustine is one of the world's best-known forts. Far less well known is a small fort to the south, Fort Matanzas. In some ways, it is more special than the larger San Marcos. It got its name from the inlet, which was the spot where the Catholic Spanish slaughtered Protestant Frenchmen in 1565. *Matanzas* means "slaughter" in Spanish. Fort Matanzas was built in 1742 to protect Matanzas Inlet, which could be used by an enemy as a backdoor entrance to St. Augustine. San Marcos was impenetrable but could be avoided by using the inlet to the south. When James Oglethorpe of Georgia used the inlet as part of his plan to blockade St. Augustine in 1740, the Spanish realized the need for an observation tower. It was built on an island—today called Rattlesnake Island—and was originally called Matanzas Tower by the Spanish. The area is marshy, and wooden pilings were used to support the thirty-foot-tall fort. The fort was nearly complete when the British under Oglethorpe tried to enter the inlet. Although only a handful of soldiers were stationed at the small fort, the cannon fire drove off scouting boats, and Oglethorpe's warship retreated without firing a shot. Fort Matanzas never fired another shot at an enemy.

As Florida passed to the British, then back to the Spanish, there was little need or desire to maintain the fort, and it fell into disrepair. U.S. soldiers never occupied it, and soon it was little more than a ruin. Although the fort had no military use, the Department of War began restoring it in 1916, and it became a national monument. For visitors, it is accessible only by boat—the National Park Service operates a small boat without charge. Once on the island, visitors can climb up the multi-level fort and see how the soldiers lived, as well as the view they saw while on patrol. On the mainland, there is a nature trail.

St. Johns County, Map 2; visit nps.gov/foma or call 305-242-7700.

FORT CLINCH

Fort Clinch on Amelia Island in Northeast Florida is a sprawling, well-preserved fort and was part of the third phase of fort construction. The Spanish first built a fortification in 1736 to protect the entrance to Cumberland Sound and the entrance to the St. Mary's River. When the Second Seminole War ended, the United States began building the fort—one of the coastal defenses that included Fort Jefferson. It is named for General Duncan Clinch, who fought in the War of 1812 and both the First and Second Seminole Wars. It is five-sided and, like the other forts, built of bricks, in this case 5 million of them. The interior structures, including a two-story barracks, are well preserved. In 1861, Confederates seized the fort and used it to protect blockade runners. But as with the other brick forts, improved weaponry made it useless. In early 1862, General Robert E. Lee ordered the fort abandoned to use its guards to meet more pressing demands. Union troops moved in and occupied it for the rest of the war.

When the Spanish-American War began in 1898, Floridians worried that the Spanish might attack. There was never a real danger, but to ease those concerns, the government stationed troops around the perimeter of Florida. The fort was activated for the first time in thirty years. Their occupation was brief, and within a few months, the fort was abandoned and deteriorated. It might have crumbled, but during the Great Depression of the 1930s, the Civilian Conservation Corps restored the fort to its Civil War–era condition. The State of Florida purchased land around the fort, acquired the fort from the federal government and created Fort Clinch State Park in 1938. During World War II, it was used by the army as a communications center and was then returned to Florida at the end of the war. It is one of the best forts to visit, and there

Fort Clinch was built on Florida's east coast but never fired a shot. It is remarkably well preserved and features frequent reenactments.

are frequent reenactments. The beach is nearby for swimming or fishing in a thousand-acre park. The fishing pier stretches half a mile into the ocean. There is also a campground with full facilities. On what is known as "First Weekend," reenactors take over, showing what it was like when the fort was occupied during the Civil War and the Spanish-American War. The demonstrations include firing the guns.

Nassau County, Map 2; for more information, visit floridastateparks.org/fortclinch or call 904-277-7274.

FORT DADE

Fort Dade—named for Major Francis Dade, who was killed during the Second Seminole War—guards the entrance to Tampa Bay. For its early history, it was more of an outpost with a lighthouse than a true fort. It first saw activity during the Third Seminole War, when captured Seminole

Indians were interned there before being moved to Oklahoma. The fort is located on a slender key, which made escape difficult for the Indians. The last group was sent west in 1858. In the first months of the Civil War, the key was seized by Confederate blockade runners but was soon taken by the Union navy. The lighthouse became a lookout for Confederate blockade runners. It also became a prison for Confederates and a sanctuary for escaped slaves and Union sympathizers.

A cemetery was established for Union and Confederate soldiers. When yellow fever swept through Key West, a U.S. Marine Hospital was established on the key to care for the sick in 1887. It became a true fort during the Spanish-American War as part of the coastal defenses established in Florida. Defenses were erected with large guns capable of sinking any Spanish ships—although none came. There are underground areas used to store shells. The marine hospital was also used for wounded soldiers. The fort saw no action, but when the war ended, work continued to expand the fortifications, with barracks and officers' quarters erected. Soon a town sprang up around the fort, with several hundred residents. During World War I, the fort was used as a training center for the National Guard. A hurricane in 1921 damaged it, including the barracks and mess hall. In 1935 and 1936, fires ravaged the area, and many buildings were razed to prevent them from burning and spreading the fires. And there were more hurricanes. The key saw more activity in World War II, when a patrol station and ammunition storage facilities were built. It became a wildlife refuge in 1974, although the Coast Guard controls the lighthouse and structures on the north end of the island. Erosion has claimed part of the island, and some of the early structures are under water.

It was actually the second Fort Dade in Florida; the first was to the north in Pasco County, built during the Second Seminole War. For a visitor seeking solitude, this is one of Florida's best parks. You will need a boat to get there, and there is no drinking water available. There are restrooms. There is ferry service to the island, operating throughout the year, although times and service vary, so check before you go (hubbardsmarina.com/Egmont-key-ferry-cruise). Remember, you have to bring everything, including food, water and sunscreen.

Pinellas County, Map 7; floridastateparks.org/parks-and-trails/Egmont-key-state-park; 772-644-6235.

FORT MOSE

Originally called Gracia Real de Santa Teresa de Mose, Fort Mose has the most unusual history of any fort in North America. In 1738, the Spanish governor of Florida built Fort Mose as the first free black settlement in North America. The Spanish had begun offering sanctuary to escaped slaves from the British colonies in 1687, and a few years later, the Spanish offered slaves freedom in Florida. That was not as generous as it might sound. First, slaves fleeing from the British colonies would create problems for the British, plus the slaves were required to convert to Catholicism and serve in the Spanish military for four years. The Spanish established the settlement north of St. Augustine, creating a first line of defense. British troops heading for St. Augustine had to pass through Fort Mose. The first military threat came in 1728, when the escaped slaves helped repulse an attack by the British. Fort Mose was a village with a wall around it and an earthen fort. As word of the fort spread to Georgia and the Carolinas, more slaves fled—or attempted to flee—to Florida. When James Oglethorpe of Georgia attacked in 1740, he laid siege to Fort Mose and captured it. The Spanish, with the help of Indian allies and black militia, counterattacked, defeated them and forced them back to Georgia. With Fort Mose destroyed, the governor moved the free blacks into St. Augustine.

The fort was rebuilt, and the free blacks returned there—some unwillingly. When the British took Florida, most of the three thousand free blacks were evacuated from Florida. The area was abandoned by the Spanish, leveled by the British and largely forgotten until 1968, when a local man used an old map to relocate the site, purchased the land and launched a campaign to excavate the land. Two decades later, Kathleen Deagan and Jane Landers wrote of the fort and its history, launching national interest. Today, there is a museum in the visitor center. In June, there is a reenactment of the Battle of Fort Mose, fought more than 250 years ago. And on the first Saturday of every month, there is musket training from 9:00 a.m. to noon. The park is open daily, but the museum is only open Thursday through Monday.

St. Johns County, Map 2; floridastateparks.org/parks-and-trails/fort-mose-historic-state-park; 804-823-2232.

FORT SAN CARLOS, BATON ROUGE

There were two Spanish forts named San Carlos—one on Amelia Island and the other in Baton Rouge. The one in Baton Rouge was originally built by the British and named Fort Richmond. When the Spanish took control of the fort in 1779, they renamed it Fort San Carlos. The Spanish divided Florida into two parts, East Florida and West Florida. East Florida consisted mostly of the peninsula, although it went farther north into present-day Georgia. West Florida today is only a shadow of what it once was. It once included what is now southern Alabama and Mississippi and eastern Louisiana. Along with Pensacola and Mobile, Baton Rouge was a major city in West Florida and protected by Fort San Carlos. Spain, once one of the mightiest nations in the world, had fallen on hard times and was unable to defend what had once been a sprawling empire. When the United States acquired the Louisiana Purchase in 1803, President Thomas Jefferson claimed that West Florida was part of the deal, a claim rejected by the Spanish. But Americans began pouring into West Florida, making the Spanish hold even weaker.

By the early 1800s, nearly all of the residents in the Baton Rouge area were Anglo-American, including Tories who had fled from the British colonies at the end of the American Revolution. Land speculators purchased property in the area, betting that the United States would acquire West Florida and land prices would soar. By 1810, revolutionary fever had taken over Baton Rouge. There were secret meetings, one of which produced calls to overthrow the Spanish. On September 23, 1810, rebels stormed Fort San Carlos, and two Spanish soldiers were killed in the battle. The rebels came prepared with their own flag: a white single star on a blue field. The revolution had begun, but there were grander plans—taking Mobile and Pensacola. The attempt to capture Mobile failed, and the idea of taking Pensacola was dropped. President James Madison wanted to intervene but felt he needed approval of Congress. Madison worried that without action by the United States, West Florida might fall to enemies of the United States. Unable to wait for Congress to act, he moved to take West Florida, even though many residents favored maintaining independence.

There were three factions competing for control: those favoring the Spanish, the Americans and the pro-independence forces. The pro-independence forces drafted a constitution and elected a governor and a legislature. Realizing the power of the Americans, the pro-independence forces surrendered and welcomed the Americans. Even today, the

Louisiana parishes that compose the Republic of West Florida are known as the "Florida Parishes."

When the Americans took most of West Florida, they gave the fort yet another new name: the Post at Baton Rouge. They erected barracks and demolished Fort San Carlos. Because of their shape, the buildings were known as the Pentagon Barracks, more than a century before the Pentagon was built outside Washington, D.C. The site was used to launch attacks against the Creek Indians and during the Civil War. The barracks was turned over to Louisiana State University for use as dormitories and today houses state offices. The barracks is on the grounds of the Louisiana Capitol, which is the site of the assassination of Senator Huey P. Long. The barrack buildings themselves are not open to the public, but visitors can walk around them. And check out the Old Arsenal Museum, which is open from Tuesday to Saturday. It is housed in an old powder magazine. And remember, it is all about 250 miles from present-day Florida, and Louisiana is not likely to give it back!

CASTILLO DE SAN MARCOS

The sprawling Castillo de San Marcos is the oldest masonry fort in the continental United States and the best known. When the Spanish landed in St. Augustine in 1565, they immediately realized the need to protect the settlement—from Indians, the French and the always expansion-minded British. The first fortifications were made of wood, but a 1668 raid by the English privateer Robert Searle destroyed much of St. Augustine and caused extensive damage to the wooden fort. The Spanish governor ordered a more substantial fort built, this one of coquina, a type of limestone made mostly from a mixture of seashells. The construction began in 1672, but the work was not completed until 1695. The fort was besieged by troops from South Carolina in 1702 and by Georgia soldiers in 1740, but both attacks failed. The new fort did its job, serving as a bulwark against invaders. When Britain gained control of Florida in 1763, the fort was renamed Fort St. Mark and then returned to its original name when Spain regained control in 1783. The United States took over Florida in 1821 and renamed it Fort Marion in honor of Revolutionary War hero Francis Marion. The United States used the fort as a prison, first for captured Seminole Indians and later for Indians from western tribes such as the Cheyennes and Apaches. The most famous prisoner was Chief Osceola,

Castillo de San Marcos National Monument, St. Augustine, Florida.

The Oldest City in the United States

Fort San Marcos was the last of several Spanish fortifications built to repel invaders. It was made of coquina, a mixture of seashells, which proved a match for cannonballs.

who came under a flag of truce but was imprisoned. He was transferred to Charleston, where he died.

In 1861, Union troops withdrew from the fort after Florida seceded from the Union. The troops left a single soldier behind as a caretaker. When the Florida militia showed up to take the fort, the soldier demanded a receipt for the fort. The fort was well armed, but the Confederacy needed the guns elsewhere. Only a handful of cannons were left at Fort Marion.

In March 1862, the USS *Wabash* arrived in the bay and found that the Confederate troops had left. City officials quickly agreed to surrender the town without a fight. It once again became a prison, this time for Union deserters and Confederates.

As the Indian wars raged in the West, the fort again housed native prisoners. Some of those housed in the fort's dungeon died there despite attempts to upgrade their living conditions. During the Spanish-American War, the fort again housed American prisoners—some two hundred deserters. Once that war ended, the military decided that the fort had no further use. In 1900, it was removed from the active rolls—it had served for more than two centuries under four flags.

The fort was transferred to the National Park Service in 1933, and in 1942, Congress restored the Spanish name Castillo de San Marcos. Throughout the day, park rangers give talks on various aspects of the fort and its history. Reenactors are frequently walking around, some carrying weapons from the Spanish period. On Fridays and Saturdays, there are historic weapons demonstrations.

St. Johns County, Map 2; for the full schedule of fort events, go to nps.gov/planyourvisit/ calendar.htm; for general information about the fort, check out nps.gov/casa or call 904- 829-6506.

FORT ZACHARY TAYLOR

Along with Fort Jefferson and Fort Clinch, Fort Zachary Taylor was one of the forts built in the mid-1800s to protect the coast of the United States. Fort Taylor is at the southern tip of Key West, a site first selected in 1822. There were delays in the construction, including a yellow fever epidemic, and construction took nearly twenty years. While it was under construction, President Zachary Taylor died, and the fort was named in his honor. The sprawling fort could house eight hundred soldiers and a large gunpowder magazine, and its five-foot-thick walls rose fifty feet above the sea. There

Fort Taylor in Key West has been occupied in every war from the Civil War to the Cuban Missile Crisis but has never seen action.

Frequent shipwrecks off the coast of Florida created a salvaging effort that made some people very wealthy and created an industry in Key West.

were forty-two guns to repel any attack from the sea. It was first used in the Civil War, when Union troops used it to keep Key West from being taken by the Confederates and to patrol for Confederate blockade runners. There were as many as forty Union warships at Key West, and they intercepted more than two hundred blockade runners. The founding of Miami was still decades away, and Key West was the largest city in Florida—it remained the largest until 1900. It was also a commercial center, the home of a nautical salvaging business that made men wealthy.

The fort was occupied during World War I and World War II and saw its final military action during the 1962 Cuban Missile Crisis. When Russian missiles were discovered in Cuba, the nation went on high alert, particularly Key West, only ninety miles from Cuba. Soldiers were sent to Key West, and although the fort itself did not play a key role, soldiers set up anti-aircraft missile launchers on the beach in front of the fort. Troops stayed at the Casa Marina Hotel. The tourists still came, and they got to see the new attraction of soldiers, missile launchers and machine guns. The best way to see Key West is on a bicycle, and the fort is designed for those who arrive on bikes or foot. As a military structure, the fort proved useless, but as a tourist destination, it is a raving success. It is a one-stop vacation with swimming, snorkeling, diving, fishing, paddling, hiking and something called Geo-seeking, a type of scavenger hunt. For those using the water or beach, there is a shower station before catching a bite in the fort's café overlooking the ocean.

Monroe County, Map 6; fortzacharytaylor.com; 305-292-6713.

NEGRO FORT

The structure was never officially named "Negro Fort," but it became known by that name. In the War of 1812, Florida was a Spanish colony, but Spain's weakness left Florida open for any army. The British built a fort to repel the Americans on the Apalachicola River in the Florida Panhandle during the war, and when the war ended in 1815, the British left and groups of free blacks, fugitive slaves and Choctaw Indians moved in. The British had a devious plan to leave the fort armed so it would cause unrest in the United States. The British commander, Edward Nicolls, knew that a fort so close to the United States would cause problems for plantation owners in nearby Alabama and Georgia. Slaves from as far away as Virginia learned of Negro Fort and the sanctuary Spanish Florida offered. It aroused the concern of the slaveholders. The *Savannah Journal* noted, "How long shall this evil, requiring immediate remedy, be permitted to exist?" The fort was not only a refuge but also a launching pad for attacks into the United States.

The United States responded by building Fort Scott on a tributary of the Apalachicola. The problem for the Americans was supplying the new fort. The easiest way was by water, but that meant traveling through Spanish territory. The Americans knew that Spain was too weak to do anything about their presence, but to reach Fort Scott, American ships had to sail by Negro Fort. The occupants of Negro Fort fired on American relief ships and killed several Americans.

On July 27, 1816, American troops attacked the fort from land and sea. Secretary of State John Quincy Adams defended the attack and quoted a letter speculating that the fort could become the basis of a slave uprising.

The attack launched the First Seminole War. There are wide estimates of how many people were in the fort. Some believe that most had fled before the attack, although others believe that there were 330 people inside Negro Fort when the attack began. They rejected calls to surrender, and the bombardment began.

A cannon shot struck the fort's powder magazine, setting off a massive explosion and instantly destroying the fort. People in Pensacola one hundred miles away heard the blast. Most of those in the fort died instantly, and others succumbed to wounds. Spain protested the presence of American troops on its soil but could do little more. Today, it is part of the Prospect Bluff Historic Sites and administered by the United States Department of Agriculture Forest Service. Visitors can see the foundations of the fort, the earthworks, a powder magazine, a cemetery and moats. Nearby are the Leon Sinks, a series of caverns and sinkholes.

Franklin County, Map 3; fs.usda.gov/recarea/Apalachicola; 850-670-8616.

10 WARS

AMERICAN REVOLUTION

Nearly every schoolchild knows of the original thirteen American colonies, but it is easy to forget that there were fifteen British colonies in 1776. Often overlooked are East Florida and West Florida, which remained loyal to King George III and worked to help the Tory cause.

The residents of Florida saw the king not as an ogre but as a great protector. The taxes the king sought in the colonies might have proved to be a burden in the thirteen other colonies, but not in Florida. The king's taxes included fees on tea and imported goods. Those living in Florida could always obtain goods from nearly Cuba or the Bahamas, and the tax on sugar imports was hardly a problem for colonies with abundant sugar.

The law that bothered the colonists outside of Florida was the Quartering Act. It required citizens to take in British soldiers, feed them and even provide them with liquor. But in Florida, the Quartering Act was embraced by citizens living on the frontier and facing challenges from the Indians. They were happy to have the British soldiers stay in their homes.

Florida attracted Scottish settlers who were loyal to the king, as well as other groups such as the Spanish, Italians, Minorcans and Greeks who had no desire to join forces with the Protestant colonies in the North.

Florida not only failed to join the Patriots but also helped the British. Florida became home to Loyalists who fled from the North and a staging ground for British troops. It was ironic that the sprawling Spanish fort that was initially built to repulse the British was instead used by the British as a base and a prison.

An influx of people and money into St. Augustine set off an economic boom, and scores of new buildings were erected. The sleepy port city became a bustling city.

While East Florida boomed as a result of the Revolution, West Florida experienced the kind of problems that would plague the colony for years. In the French and Indian War, Spain had allied with France, and when France lost, Spain turned Florida over to the victorious British. In the American Revolution, Spain allied with the Patriots in 1779.

The Spanish saw a way to reclaim the two Floridas, or at the very least West Florida. The Spanish controlled Louisiana and used it as a base to attack British West Florida. They began by attacking Fort Bute, an outpost on the Mississippi River, and then moved to take Baton Rouge and Mobile. British reinforcements finally arrived to defend Pensacola, its final outpost in West Florida. The British also had the support of many of the Native Americans, including more than 1,500 who came to defend Pensacola, but most drifted away. The Spanish laid siege to the city, and after several battles, the British surrendered the city. The Spanish controlled West Florida after they threatened British colonies in the Caribbean.

The British retained East Florida throughout the war, but after General Cornwallis surrendered in 1783, they realized it was too difficult and expensive to defend. Thousands of British supporters—including escaped slaves—were evacuated to the Bahamas, Jamaica, Canada or back to England. It was not the last time British troops would march in Florida.

Throughout the war, Patriots made raids into Florida, but there was only one battle, at Thomas Creek in Nassau County in 1777. Troops from the Continental army and Georgia militias were repulsed by the British Regular Army. It was the southernmost battle of the American Revolution. There is a historic marker in Callahan. Bernardo de Galvez was the Spanish governor of Louisiana who aided the Patriots during the Revolution. In 2018, a statue of De Galvez was unveiled in downtown Pensacola. Galvez Day is celebrated in Pensacola each May 8 and includes a series of events. There is a historic marker on West La Rua Street in Pensacola.

WAR OF 1812

As the War of 1812 began, Spain chose to support Britain against the United States. They hoped that Britain might help them hold on to Florida, which was under increasing pressure from the United States.

The Spanish allowed Britain to build a fort on the Apalachicola River and occupy Pensacola. The town became a haven for runaway slaves and Indians. Britain used Florida to gather its troops, which made Florida a target for General Andrew Jackson and his troops. On November 7, 1814, Jackson attacked Pensacola and forced the British out of the city.

The British troops fled to a nearby fort but were quickly routed and blew up the fort before fleeing. Jackson was poised to take all of Florida from the Spanish, although he lacked the authority for his invasion. It might have happened, but Jackson received word of British activity near New Orleans, dropped his plans for Florida and headed west for the final battle of the War of 1812.

The British also picked up support from the Red Stick Creek tribe, who moved into Alabama, attacked near Mobile and massacred hundreds of people. Jackson responded by attacking two Indian villages and then fought the Battle of Horseshoe Bend, which ended with a final defeat of the tribe and the end of its power in Alabama and Georgia. The tribe surrendered 23 million acres.

Spain had already lost most of West Florida in 1810, and the War of 1812 left its position in the remaining territory untenable. Each year, Spain grew weaker. Even before the war, it depended on the British navy to protect the east coast. As the British ships sailed away, the coast became a camping ground for pirates and adventurers. Spain watched helplessly as events spun out of its control and its options decreased.

One of the smaller battles of the War of 1812 took place at Waterman's Bluff when Georgia militia invaded Florida and settled on the plantation of Eleazar Waterman. Spanish troops attacked but were repulsed by the Americans in Yulee. There is a historic marker to mark the battle.

FIRST SEMINOLE WAR

By 1816, Spain had lost control of Florida. The Seminole Indians established their base in West Florida and could strike into Georgia or Alabama at will, moving back to Spanish Florida. At the same time, plantation owners from Georgia and Alabama struck into North Florida seeking their runaway slaves. The Seminoles were reinforced by escaped slaves from plantations in the United States and aided by British traders who sold them guns.

In 1817, Andrew Jackson received command of United States forces in the region and moved into Florida with three thousand soldiers, destroying

Seminole villages and seizing a Spanish fort at St. Marks. He executed two British traders who were aiding the Seminoles and then turned to familiar ground: Pensacola.

He captured the Spanish fort in Pensacola and deposed the government. Although Jackson had won major victories against the Seminoles, they remained a force, and it would take two more wars to neutralize the Seminoles, although they would never be defeated.

SECOND SEMINOLE WAR

Once Andrew Jackson became president in 1829, the fate of the Seminole Indians in Florida was sealed. As settlers moved into Florida, problems with Indians multiplied, and Jackson wanted them moved out of Florida and shipped west. In 1832, the Treaty of Payne's Landing supposedly provided for the Seminoles to go west within three years, and by 1834, nearly four thousand Indians had made the move. The circumstances of the treaty signing were murky and questionable. But thousands more, led by Chief Osceola, refused to go. He vowed to fight to the death.

Three days after Christmas 1835, Osceola attacked and killed the Indian agent General Wiley Thompson near Ocala. Miles away, some three hundred Seminoles ambushed Major Francis Dade, killing all but three of his soldiers.

In 1837, there was a truce and negotiations began. The "negotiations" were a trick, and Osceola was captured and jailed at St. Augustine and then Fort Moultrie in Charleston. He died there in 1838. The truce ended, and his followers continued the fight, although it became a war of attrition.

In December 1837, future president Zachary Taylor was leading his soldiers to Lake Okeechobee to find Seminoles. On Christmas Day, Taylor and his 1,100 soldiers were attacked by about 400 Seminoles. Taylor and his soldiers were forced to withdraw.

With the costs mounting and the task of rounding up the Indians seemingly impossible, the United States ended the fighting—for a time. Thousands of Seminoles died, 4,400 surrendered and were sent to Oklahoma and only about 500 Seminoles remained, primarily hiding out in the Everglades. Some 1,500 soldiers died.

THIRD SEMINOLE WAR

The third and final war between the United States and the Seminoles was the most senseless. By the 1850s, the Seminoles were living peacefully in South Florida and growing crops. The trouble began when Colonel William Harney arrived with a surveying crew and decided to provoke Seminole chief Billy Bowlegs, even though Harney was under orders not to provoke the Indians. Bowlegs had cultivated a large banana plantation, and one night Harney and his surveyors trashed his crop. The surveyors admitted responsibility and treated it as a joke, saying that they wanted "to see old Billy cut up." The army refused to apologize or offer compensation, and many believe that the surveying crew was sent to provoke the Indians into a war. Some forty followers of Bowlegs attacked the army camp and killed four soldiers. An army force outnumbering the Indians fourteen to one was sent to retaliate. In 1857, the army destroyed Bowlegs's camp, and the soldiers took the tribe's corn, rice and oxen. The raid brought Bowlegs to the conference table.

The United States offered bribes ranging from $7,500 for Bowlegs to $500 for each warrior and $100 for each woman and child. Most of the Indians accepted the offer—including Bowlegs—and moved to Oklahoma. But about two hundred to three hundred Seminoles refused to move, forming the nucleus of what is today the Seminole tribe. The final Seminole War came to an end, but within two years, Florida would be plunged into another war.

CIVIL WAR

Even before the 1860 election, it was clear how Florida felt about Abraham Lincoln. State officials refused to put his name on the ballot. They also kept Stephen Douglas, the official Democratic Party nominee, off the ballot, giving voters the choice of just two southern candidates.

When Lincoln won, Florida leaders began talking about leaving the Union. South Carolina was first to leave. Florida governor John Milton called a convention, and Florida became the third state to leave—one day after Mississippi. There were a few voices of warning, including former governor Richard Keith Call, who said, "You have opened the gates of Hell, from which shall flow the curses of the damned which shall sink you to perdition."

Fort San Marcos in St. Augustine was occupied briefly by the Confederates in the Civil War before being retaken by Union troops.

There was no Confederacy when Florida left, so it briefly became an independent nation with a single-star flag. It didn't last long. Florida delegates went to Montgomery to help form the Confederate States of America. Milton moved quickly to seize Federal armories in St. Augustine, Chattahoochee and Fernandina. Union troops abandoned two forts in Pensacola, but to the dismay of the Confederates, they held the third fort on nearby Santa Rosa Island. It was not much of a fort, unoccupied for more than a dozen years, but the Union held it until the end of the war.

With the North and South looking at each other from opposing forts, many thought that the Civil War would begin in Florida. There were shots exchanged, but the real fighting began at Fort Sumter in South Carolina. Florida was the smallest state in the Confederacy, with a population of 140,000, nearly half of whom were slaves. A New York newspaper called Florida the "smallest tadpole in the dirty pool of secession."

There was a rush to enlist: nearly 7,000 in the first three months—2,000 more than the government had asked for. Still, 2,300 Floridians enlisted in the Union army and navy, about half of them slaves.

Florida played a major role in Lincoln's plan to isolate the South, the Anaconda Plan. The plan was to blockade the Southern ports, preventing cotton from leaving the United States and preventing guns and ammunition from entering. Because of its long coastline, Florida was a smugglers' paradise, and the Union navy dedicated most of its resources to ports in Charleston, Norfolk and New Orleans.

Florida was of little value military value to the North or South, but it was important for its crops, cattle and salt. In the early days of the war, thousands of cows were sold to the Confederacy, and salt-making plants were set up along the coast. Salt was so vital that salt makers were exempted from the draft. As the war dragged on, the South ran out of money, and the Florida cattlemen were reluctant to surrender their cows for promises of future payment or Confederate money. The salt plants on the coast became frequent targets of Union patrols.

Only one major battle was fought in Florida during the Civil War, the ill-fated Battle of Olustee. Union troops hoped to bring Florida back into the Union in time for the 1864 election, but the army was routed in one of the last major victories for the Confederates.

The only major battle in Florida took place in 1864 when Union troops moved into Florida from their base in Jacksonville. As the Union troops approached Lake City, then the largest city between Jacksonville and the Panhandle, Confederate forces from Georgia and Florida stopped their advance at Olustee and sent the Union troops fleeing to Jacksonville. It was a complete rout.

At the end of the war, Tallahassee was the only capital east of the Mississippi still in Confederate hands. The war's toll on Florida was staggering: of the fifteen thousand who went to war, five thousand were killed, thousands more were wounded and nearly every family in the state was touched by the war.

Each year in February, there is a reenactment of the Battle of Olustee. The battlefield is isolated, and be sure to consult the website for details about parking and transportation (battleofolustee.org/reenactment.html). The Olustee Battlefield Historic State Park is open throughout the year. It is located about fifty miles west of Jacksonville. (See floridastateparks.org/parks-and-trails/olustee-battlefield-historic-state-park.)

SPANISH-AMERICAN WAR

Even before Ponce de León came to Florida, there were indications that natives from Cuba had contact with tribes in Florida. As Spain conquered large portions of the New World, Havana became its center. Even today, the records of early Florida are housed in archives in Cuba. As both Cuba and the United States grew, people moved between the two.

The unsuccessful Cuban Revolution of 1868 sent thousands of Cubans fleeing to the United States, settling primarily in Key West, Tampa or New York. In Tampa and Key West, they established the cigar industry. The center of cigar manufacturing was Ybor City in Tampa.

The factories produced more than cigars—they created a center of militant anti-Spanish activity and financing for another revolution. Cigar workers contributed a portion of their pay to a fund to finance the revolution, and plans for the revolt were smuggled inside cigars.

While the Cuban revolutionaries saw Florida as a staging ground for a new revolution, Floridians were not so sure. They worried that if there was a war involving the United States, Spain might attack Florida—the closest state. There were also economic considerations. Florida worried that if the United States helped Cubans gain independence from Spain, the island might become a state and compete economically with Florida. To please

Thousands of Cuban exiles streamed into Ybor City to work in the cigar factories. At the upper right, sitting above the workers, is the lector. He was hired by the cigar workers to spend the day reading to them from newspapers, books and magazines.

Floridians, Congress passed legislation promising that the United States would not acquire Florida and stationed troops around the perimeter of the state. Miami was a new town in 1898, but soldiers were stationed there in case of a Spanish invasion. Once victory was assured, the camps in Miami and Fernandina were closed.

Although Floridians worried that a war with Spain would hurt the state, it proved to be a boon. The War Department set up its headquarters in Tampa, and thousands of men and tons of supplies poured into the city. At one point, trains carrying military supplies were backed up nearly one hundred miles from Tampa to Ocala. The military set up headquarters in the elegant Tampa Bay Hotel, while twenty-five thousand soldiers camped anywhere a tent could be pitched. Once the city was full, troops were sent to Lakeland to camp.

On June 14, 1898, sixteen thousand troops jammed on thirty-five ships for the trip to Cuba.

The Key West Cemetery holds the graves of a number of sailors killed in the explosion of the USS *Maine* in Havana Harbor in 1898. Nearby, the Key West Museum at the Custom House houses the courtroom where the navy held an inquiry into the sinking of the *Maine*. In Tampa, Hotel Tampa Bay was the headquarters for the American soldiers. Fort De Soto in Pinellas County was in use during the war, although it never fired a shot.

WORLD WAR I

When the United States entered World War I in 1917, Florida had the smallest population in the South—fewer than 1 million people. Of the 4 million men who served during the war, just 42,030 were from Florida, about one-third of whom were African American. By the end of the war, 1,134 Floridians were killed.

Florida's greatest contribution to the war came in the air. After the Wright brothers first flew, the debate began over whether airplanes could be used in war. There were plenty of doubters. Despite the work of the Wright brothers, the United States lagged behind France and Britain in developing planes for war. As World War I began, the military found that Florida was the perfect place to train pilots. Good weather year-round and plenty of open space for airfields were major attractions.

The navy established an aviation school in Pensacola in 1914—the same year war broke out in Europe—and Glenn Curtiss established his own school near Miami in 1917 to train marine pilots during the war. The Marine Corps even made a movie in Miami, *Flying with the Marines*, which was shown in theaters around the nation. A Naval Air Station was established at Key West; it trained five hundred airmen during the war.

Pensacola had been the site of forts for three hundred years and had seen invading armies from five nations. Camp Joe Johnson was established for the Florida National Guard, but when the war began, the United States government took over. It grew to six hundred buildings and at its height had a population of nearly twenty-seven thousand.

In Arcadia, Carlstrom Field and Door Field trained pilots, and Arcadia became known as "Aviation City." At the same time, Charles Kettering and Lawrence Sperry conducted unsuccessful tests on a new weapon: guided missiles.

In Key West, Thomas Edison worked on what became known as depth bombs, as well as other devices that met with varying degrees of success. In Jacksonville, a large shipbuilding plant built twenty-three steamships, while Tampa firms built twenty-eight ships.

Suspicion of anything German grew in Florida. People called hamburgers "liberty sandwiches," and sauerkraut became "liberty cabbage." There was even a call for an investigation of Edward Conradi, the president of Florida State College for Women, because his parents were German.

The National Naval Aviation Museum (navalaviationmuseum.org) in Pensacola features more than 150 aircraft dating back to World War I. The sprawling museum covers nearly seven acres of display space. It is open daily and admission is free.

WORLD WAR II

When Henry Flagler and his wealthy friends began coming to Florida in the late 1800s, they stayed for what became known as "the Season." They brought their servants and trunks full of clothing and stayed for months during the winter.

Vacation patterns had changed by 1941, but the Season was still something Floridians looked forward to. As it approached, there was speculation about how many tourists would come and how many hotel rooms would be filled. The Great Depression ravaged Florida's economy, and by 1941, the tourist comeback was complete. Traditionally, the Season began on the first Sunday in December. Just as room clerks welcomed guests on December 7, Japanese planes were bombing Pearl Harbor.

Even before the bombs fell on Pearl Harbor, the military presence in Florida was growing. Britain desperately needed pilots to hold back the German *Luftwaffe*, but the skies over England were not safe for pilot training, so the British government turned to the United States. Some 1,500 British airmen underwent training in Arcadia and Clewiston.

As soon as Germany declared war on the United States, its submarines headed for Florida for Operation Drumbeat. The goal was to sink oil tankers coming from Texas to the East Coast. As they sailed up the coast of Florida, the submarines waited offshore and fired their deadly torpedoes. Over a ten-day period, a tanker went down every day. In Key West, a blimp was shot down by a submarine.

The Nazis sank twenty-four ships, and President Roosevelt ordered patrol torpedo boats (PT boats) quickly built to repel the submarines.

About 250,000 Floridians served in the military, and 3,000 died. But the biggest impact on Florida was not the number that left Florida to serve, but rather the number that came to Florida to train. About 2 million men and women from every branch trained in Florida, including two future presidents, John F. Kennedy and George H.W. Bush.

As for the Miami hotel owners, they quickly found new occupants for their hotel rooms: thousands of soldiers who came to train. It was a strange contrast. Some soldiers were living in luxury in Miami hotel rooms, while others were living in crude, quickly built barracks in Camp Blanding, Fort Pierce or a dozen other cities.

The war had a lasting impact. People who came for military training stayed or decided to come back when they retired. The state's population soared 46 percent between 1940 and 1950 to 2,771,305.

Thousands of soldiers filled Miami hotel rooms during World War II. Here, soldiers march through downtown as part of their training.

Monuments to World War II abound in Florida. The Camp Gordon Johnston Museum in Carabelle features displays centered on the amphibious soldiers who trained in Franklin County. Each March, the museum features Camp Gordon Johnson Reunion Days (see campgordonjohnson.com). There is a museum and park at Camp Blanding near Starke. Camp Blanding became the largest army base in Florida. The museum is open daily from noon to 4:00 p.m. and is free (see campblanding-museum.org). And the best military museum in Florida, the Pensacola Naval Air Station Museum, has elaborate World War II displays. There are a number of other places where you can learn about Florida's role in World War II. (Check out dos.myflorida.com/historical/preservation/heritage-trails/world-war-ii-heritage-trail.)

TWENTY-FIRST-CENTURY WARS

Americans generally think of the Pentagon in suburban Washington, D.C., when they think of military command. Little known is the USCENTCOM in Tampa, which directs American military operations in the Middle East and Central Asia. When it was established, few realized that all of America's future military conflicts would fall under CENTCOM. From the Horn of Africa to Central Asia, CENTCOM has responsibility for some of the most dangerous places in the world.

Tampa has a long history of military involvement, beginning with the Seminole Wars in the 1800s. The town began as Fort Brooke, a military outpost, and in 1898 became the embarkation point for the Spanish-American War.

In 1939, as war in Europe loomed, the State of Florida gave the federal government land for an air base, and it was named for Colonel Leslie MacDill, who died in a 1938 plane crash. During the Cuban Missile Crisis, the United States Strike Command was established at MacDill.

CENTCOM's first fight came in 1991, when Iraq invaded Kuwait, and the United States responded with military force. Operation Desert Storm was a quick and decisive fight, and Kuwait was quickly freed. Following the terrorist attacks of 9/11, the United States invaded Iraq under Operation Iraqi Freedom (2003–11) and the Afghanistan War, which began in 2001.

MacDill is closed to the public but does conduct weekly tours for small groups, usually on Thursday. The four-hour tour fills up quickly, and it is best to sign up early. Contact the MacDill public relations office for details (macdill.af.mil).

10 HURRICANES

1559

Spanish King Philip II wanted his nation to settle the east and west coasts of Florida, and in 1559, he sent Tristán de Luna with thirteen ships, two hundred horses and 1,500 settlers and soldiers. There were even 200 Aztecs from Mexico. They arrived in present-day Pensacola to establish the first permanent settlement in the New World. Within weeks, history was changed. De Luna was to establish his headquarters and then push inland to claim much of the Southeast and travel east to present-day Parris Island, South Carolina. They began clearing the land, laying out streets and lots and building homes. A ship was sent to Spain to report on the success of the mission.

Four weeks after they landed, a devastating hurricane passed through the Caribbean and struck Pensacola without warning. The storm broke ships apart, and the captain of the fleet's flagship, *Jesus*, drowned. The storm destroyed nearly all the supplies. Just one ship was left intact, but it was washed ashore and ended up in a grove of trees.

The death toll is unknown, but at least five hundred people died, leaving De Luna to care for one thousand survivors. Two hundred men were sent inland to look for supplies, and ships were dispatched to Havana and Veracruz for help. For two years, the settlers tried to turn a disaster into success, but in 1561, the king canceled the expedition. Had it succeeded, the history of North America could have been quite different.

1919

It was not until the 1950s that hurricanes gained names, beginning with words from the Army/Navy Phonetic Library—Able, Baker, Charlie—and then moving to women's names in 1953, with the addition of men's names coming in 1979. Before then, hurricanes were given descriptive names after the fact, such as the Great Hurricane of 1919. Even today, it remains one of the largest storms to hit North America. It did not come within one hundred miles of the Florida peninsula, but it did massive damage to the Florida Keys, striking with little warning. When the weather station at Miami finally received warning of an approaching storm, winds were already picking up. The storm passed through the Straits of Florida, pounding the Keys. The storm moved slowly, intensifying the damage. The winds only reached one hundred miles an hour, but they lasted for nearly forty hours. It was the third-most intense storm of the twentieth century until Hurricane Andrew in 1992 pushed it into fourth place.

The storm left the Keys and moved into the Gulf of Mexico, heading to the Texas coast, where it struck Corpus Christi, killing nearly three hundred. The greatest death toll came at sea, where dozens of ships went down. The

The hurricane of 1919 did extensive damage to the Sand Key Lighthouse.

Corydon sank, taking twenty-seven men, but the greatest toll came from the mysterious sinking of the *Valbanera*, a steamship that started from Spain with one thousand passengers. As the hurricane approached, half the passengers became worried and got off in Santiago, Cuba. The ship reached Havana as the winds picked up and decided to wait offshore for rough seas to subside.

The ship was never heard from again, and its fate remains a mystery today. It was found a week later with its mast sticking up about forty miles west of Key West. The ship was intact, and the lifeboats had never been lowered.

1926

As the city of Miami celebrated its thirtieth birthday, the city's future seemed unlimited, but disaster and an economic depression were just one storm away. By 1926, the mangrove fields of Miami Beach were gone, replaced with ever larger hotels. In Miami, empty fields became subdivisions, and once worthless pieces of land went for thousands of dollars.

There were problems. The housing boom created shortages of building materials, and shantytowns sprang up around Miami. The boom turned into a bust because of what was called the Great Miami Hurricane.

As with many other storms during the era, the Miami Weather Bureau had little information as the storm approached. The storm came ashore at night, and finally the Weather Bureau raised a red-and-black flag to indicate a hurricane, but too late. The wind increased to about 140 miles per hour. The winds woke up most of the sleeping residents and quickly blew away the shanty towns. Instruments to measure the weather were blown away, leaving forecasters to guess at how bad it was.

The water rushed into downtown Miami, and there was a traffic jam caused by boats pushed ashore. As the eye of the storm came ashore, people jumped into cars to escape, but when the eye passed, the rest of the storm came ashore with more fury than the first half. Cars on the causeway between Miami Beach and Miami were blown away.

The two cities were in ruins. A reporter from the *Miami Tribune* reached West Palm Beach and told the world of the disaster. The damage was even worse inland. The town of Moore Haven, on the banks of Lake Okeechobee, was submerged in as much as fifteen feet of water, and residents survived by clinging to roofs. Bodies were swept into the Everglades and never seen again—or counted in the death toll. The damage spread as far north as Cocoa Beach.

The storm moved into the Gulf of Mexico and went ashore on the Florida-Alabama border. The storm nearly destroyed the waterfront, and as with Miami, boats were washed into city streets. Funeral homes became crowded with bodies, but the city was too busy to worry about funerals. The Florida East Coast Railway, the primary north–south conduit for the state, offered free passage for those who wanted to leave the state—and thousands took the offer. Martial law was declared, and a dozen people were shot for looting. The official death toll passed one thousand, although the total will never be known.

The storm marked the death of the Florida land boom. Land prices had soared up until the day the storm struck. Afterward, they fell dramatically—a lot that went for $60,000 was sold for $600. Thousands of people had put down small down payments, and after the storm, they simply abandoned their properties. Many who were considering buying land saw what a hurricane could do and changed their minds.

For the rest of the nation, the Great Depression began in 1929, but in Florida, it started in 1926 as dozens of banks failed. They had lent money to the land buyers and found themselves with millions of dollars in bad debts. A hurricane two years later finished what was left of the boom.

1928

The major storm of 1928, known as the Great Okeechobee Flood, was the deadliest to strike Florida. Guesses of the death toll in Florida range from 1,830 to 3,500. The storm passed through the Caribbean, devastating Guadeloupe, St. Kitts, Puerto Rico and Montserrat, and 1,500 were already dead by the time the storm reached Palm Beach. The winds hit 150 miles an hour, and nearly twenty inches of rain fell on West Palm Beach. Thousands of homes were destroyed from Miami to Fort Pierce.

Newspapers around the nation carried headlines such as "Florida Destroyed." The early reports came from the coast, and it took time for reports to come in from around Lake Okeechobee. Moore Haven, on the lake's west bank, had been nearly destroyed by the 1926 hurricane, and just as it was coming back, the 1928 hurricane struck. The storm washed away communities on the southern shore as the waters from the lake rushed over the land. In the darkness, people could not be sure where to run. People climbed trees seeking safety, or as the waters mounted, they grabbed onto trees as they floated by.

The death toll from the 1928 hurricane will never be known. Hundreds of coffins were sent to areas around Lake Okeechobee, but most of the bodies were buried in mass graves.

The worst of the storm hit Belle Glade. People took refuge in homes and watched as the waters began to rise around them. They moved to tabletops and then to the rafters and finally to rooftops. A woman tied herself to a telegraph pole and survived. As the eye passed over, many believed that the worst was over, venturing out to survey the damage. When the storm struck again, they were washed away.

Lake Okeechobee was cut off from civilization, and it took three days for the governor to learn what had happened at the fourth-largest lake in the United States. The search for bodies began immediately, but as with the 1926 storm, many were washed into the Everglades and never found. After six weeks, the search was abandoned.

After the storm passed, hundreds of people walked forty miles to West Palm Beach to seek medical help and food. The stench of death hung in the air as bodies of people, alligators, fish and other animals piled up. At first there were attempts to provide individual coffins, but the task was overwhelming and officials turned to mass graves—one held 1,600 bodies.

One of the strangest stories to come from the storm involved Deputy State Hotel Commissioner Pat Houston, who went missing and was suspected of robbing the commission. He was cleared when his body was found.

The 1926 hurricane brought the state disastrous publicity and killed the land boom. In the wake of the 1928 storm, state officials initially decided to downplay the destruction to prevent more bad publicity. They told the world that it was not that bad, but this only delayed relief efforts.

1935

When Hurricane Katrina struck New Orleans, President George W. Bush suffered a significant blow to his popularity when his administration was seen as failing to respond adequately. It was not the first time a president was blamed for the lack of response to a hurricane. The first was Franklin D. Roosevelt in 1935, who was blamed for the deaths of scores of veterans in a scathing article by Ernest Hemingway.

The Great Depression left millions without jobs, including tens of thousands of veterans from World War I. Many took part in a march on Washington, known as the Bonus March, to demand their World War I bonus. When Roosevelt became president in 1933, he initiated job programs, including one that employed hundreds of veterans—some from the Bonus March—who were sent to the Florida Keys to work on building projects. They lived in tents or small shacks in the Keys alongside the road they were building.

On Labor Day weekend in 1935, a hurricane approached the Keys, but no one seemed concerned about the safety of the veterans. The Weather Bureau was of little help, predicting a hurricane with "probably winds of hurricane force." With a long holiday weekend approaching, few paid any attention to the story that seemed to hold little threat.

The Weather Bureau failed to predict the increasing strength, and when it finally came ashore, it was one of the strongest storms on record. It struck Long Key and Lower Matecumbe Key and destroyed the instruments used to measure the wind speed. The best estimate is that winds reached 150 to 200 miles per hour. The storm created a massive storm tide that drowned hundreds and leveled the middle Keys.

The manager of the veterans' camp on Upper Matecumbe Key repeatedly called the Miami Weather Bureau for details, and as the reports became more ominous, he wired the Florida East Coast Railway to send the train that had been promised. Some people fled the key, but others waited patiently for the train. The railway had promised to have a train standing by, but it was a lie. There were delays caused by difficulty finding workers on a holiday weekend.

It was nearly 5:00 p.m. before the train finally left Miami, but then it encountered more delays. It was already raining when the train first reached the Keys, and debris on the tracks caused more delays. By 8:00 p.m., the train was in the midst of the hurricane. A giant wave struck the train and sent ten of its cars off the tracks, scattering them like so many toys. The water was high enough to put out the fire in the engine.

The 1935 hurricane was so powerful it blew a rescue train off the tracks, scattering the cars like toys.

The veterans were exposed to the worst of the storm and had nowhere to run. The death toll is at best an educated guess. Some were swept out to sea, and because of concerns about disease and the overwhelming number of bodies, many were buried in unmarked graves or cremated. On the north bank of a creek, dozens of pine caskets were covered with fuel and

Most people thought it could not be done, but Henry Flagler built his railroad from Miami to Key West.

burned. A volunteer played taps on a bugle. Some of the vets had gone to Miami for the holiday weekend, and their fate became a question mark for those trying to identify the missing. One estimate is that 257 veterans and 259 others died.

The finger-pointing began immediately. Hemingway came up from his Key West home to take part in rescue efforts as soon as the storm passed. He wrote a scathing article, "Who Murdered the Vets?" placing the blame on Roosevelt. Roosevelt ordered an inquiry and worked to deflect blame. There was a Congressional investigation that, in the end, blamed the hurricane rather than any of the individuals involved.

Flagler's magnificent railroad through the Keys was in ruins, with large portions washed away and tracks twisted. The railroad had gone into bankruptcy as a result of the Great Depression and the bust of the Florida land boom. The remains of the railroad to the Keys was turned into a highway.

1947

The hurricane season of 1947 was brutal for Florida. During World War II, military forecasters in the Pacific gave names to storm to keep them straight, and when they returned to their civilian jobs, they continued to use names, although they were not disclosed to the public. The first of the bad storms struck on September 17—the Weather Bureau nicknamed it "George"—with Category 4 intensity. Its winds raged from Miami to Cape Canaveral. It moved slowly across the state and caused flooding from Miami to Naples, and its 150-mile-per-hour wind gusts caused widespread destruction in Fort Lauderdale and Hollywood.

Once it reached the Gulf of Mexico, it began to regain strength and headed to New Orleans, where it caused even greater damage along the Louisiana-Mississippi coast. The death toll was remarkably low in Florida, fewer than twenty. Four weeks later, a second storm struck—this one nicknamed "King"—but came from the west, through the Keys and exiting the East Coast. The winds were not that bad—about ninety miles per hour—but the heavy rain did extensive damage, flooding streets throughout South Florida. In Hialeah, the waters were waist deep, even worse than the 1926 storm. Thousands of people were homeless, and throughout Miami, small boats became the preferred mode of transportation.

The first large postwar hurricanes produced some strange theories. One was that the atomic bomb might be used to destroy a hurricane, and another urged the seeding of a hurricane with dry ice. General

Homes along the Gulf Coast suffered extensive damage from the 1950 hurricane.

Electric scientists joined with the government to test the dry ice theory out in 1947 after the second hurricane entered the Atlantic Ocean and seemed to be heading far out into the Atlantic Ocean. A military plane dropped eighty pounds of dry ice over the storm. The outcome was not what scientists anticipated. The storm stalled, moved back to the United States and came ashore near Savannah. Floods spread as far north as Charleston. At least one scientist thought that the dry ice brought the storm back to the United States, and it discouraged seeding for nearly twenty years.

1950'S EASY

This was the year the government began assigning names to hurricanes, at first utilizing the Army/Navy Phonetic Alphabet. The storms to strike Florida had the inappropriate name "Easy" and the appropriate name "King."

Easy turned out to be the most unusual storm to land in Florida. It came from Cuba and moved near Key West with minimal winds. Newspapers called it a "Baby Hurricane," easily dismissed. It moved along the west coast and swept high tides onto the coast. By the time it reached Tampa Bay, the Baby Hurricane was turning into a real threat. Then the strangeness began. It moved past Tampa, slowed and stopped west of Tarpon Springs. Winds increased to 125 miles per hour as it sat offshore and formed a loop before moving ashore near Cedar Key, which had already endured a vicious pounding.

Then it turned north, formed a loop and moved inland, turning south a bit and heading for Jacksonville. Cedar Key received twenty-four inches of rain before the gauge overflowed, and other areas recorded thirty inches. The worst was at Yankeetown, where thirty-nine inches fell in twenty-four hours. Cedar Key was a mess, with roofs flying off three out of four homes in the town. The town's fishing fleet, which was the lifeblood of the community, was destroyed. The docks were in ruins, and the fish houses on shore were leveled.

1960'S DONNA

Donna became one of the deadliest storms in history, killing people in Puerto Rico, the Bahamas and the United States. In the Keys, the storm reminded residents of the 1935 storm, and many fled. When the storm

Hurricane Donna was one of the deadliest hurricanes in history, with 150-mile-per-hour winds.

struck the islands in the dead of night, the winds were 150 miles an hour, and those who stayed soon wished they had left.

The storm was so powerful that it washed out parts of the Overseas Highway. The pipe bringing fresh water to the Keys broke in six places. Homes floated away and ended up in scores of places—out in the ocean, on the Overseas Highway or blocks from where they started.

As dawn came, people left the schools, churches and buildings where they had sought shelter and surveyed the damage. Many were in shock, having survived hours of deafening wind and then finding everything they owned washed away. Marines were brought in to patrol the streets, and the navy sent crews to fix the water pipeline.

The storm moved into the Everglades, where it killed hundreds of thousands of birds, including the rare great white herons, whose population was nearly cut in half. Hundreds of magnificent mangroves and mahogany trees fell, including many that survived the 1935 storm. Most residents of Everglades City evacuated as the storm approached, so when floodwaters came rushing in, only a few hundred people were left to flee to higher ground.

It was almost the end for Everglades City. After the storm was finished with the town, the county moved the county seat to Naples, and the Collier Company moved its headquarters.

The storm caused widespread destruction along the west coast to Fort Myers and Naples and then turned northeast, pushed through the center of the state and exited at Jacksonville. It continued its path of destruction up the East Coast of the United States, causing havoc all the way to New England. It took weeks to tally up the toll: thirteen people were dead in Florida, 1,844 homes were destroyed and more than 3,000 had major damage. The storm caused disaster along the East Coast as far north as Caribou, Maine. Florida began to dig out. It was classified as the sixth-worst storm to strike the United States.

1992'S ANDREW

Often people talk about hurricanes as the "Big One." If there was ever a Big One in Florida, it was Andrew, which struck South Florida and left the entire region reeling. With wind gusts of 175 miles an hour, the storm landed south of Miami and was so vicious that it took weeks to tally the damage. The storm revealed weak construction standards and even construction fraud.

People fled—the estimates run as high as 700,000—and jammed the highways heading north. As with many storms, it struck at night, and those who remained in their homes could only wait and hope.

There was some hope, as it was a small hurricane by the standards of the major storms and seemed to lack the precipitation of other storms. And it was moving quickly—it moved across the state in three hours.

The worst of the storm missed Miami, although there was wind damage there, but it struck places people had never heard of: Cutler Ridge, Florida City and Homestead. In Homestead, the damage was close to total; even Homestead Air Force Base, the economic lifeline of the city, was leveled. The sustained winds appeared to be 145 miles per hour, but gusts of 175 miles per hour were recorded.

Many homes seemed to disintegrate, and people struggled to find the exact spot where their home once stood. Barometer readings established the storm as the third most intense to hit the United States in the twentieth century.

At the National Weather Center in Coral Gables, steel window coverings were in place, but the winds blew the giant radar dome off the roof and onto the ground. The weather center barely maintained contact with the outside world.

The damage caused by Hurricane Andrew around Homestead was the most destructive in Florida history.

The numbers are staggering: eighty thousand homes suffered extensive damage or were destroyed, and forty-four deaths were attributed to the storm. Eleven insurance companies went bankrupt, swamped by more than 600,000 insurance claims.

The storm led to significant revisions in the state's building codes. A statewide building code was adopted, eliminating the hodgepodge of local regulations and establishing statewide standards. The new code worked, and studies showed that damage in subsequent hurricanes was dramatically lower in structures built under the new codes.

2004'S CHARLEY

Florida had never seen anything like it. In the previous 450 years, the state had experienced hundreds of hurricanes, but it never saw a year such as 2004. Within six weeks, four storms swept through the state.

The first was Charley, which arrived at Port Charlotte on the west coast on August 13 with 150-mile-per-hour winds. It had seemed like a serious but not catastrophic storm, but as it approached the coast, its wind speeds increased from 115 miles per hour to 145 miles per hour and its path changed from a sure landing in the Tampa Bay area to a north-by-northwest track. The dramatic change left many people unprepared.

Francis followed, landing on the opposite coast near Palm Beach with 140-mile-per-hour winds. Ivan struck the Panhandle with 120-mile-per-hour winds, and finally Jeanne followed the path established by Francis, which was still recovering from the earlier storm. But the worst was Charley, which struck with 150-mile-per-hour winds when it came ashore on the southwest coast and moved swiftly toward the northeast, arriving in Orlando in midafternoon with 85-mile-an-hour winds and then heading out to the Atlantic before sunset. The storm took just seven hours to travel from Captiva Island to Daytona Beach.

In the small town of Arcadia, 3,500 were people crowded into the town's only shelter when the wind blew the roof off. Nine out of ten buildings in the downtown area were damaged. Small towns such as Lake Wales, Avon Park and Sebring suffered some of the worst damage. It was difficult to recognize Punta Gorda and Port Charlotte as cities anymore. Throughout the state, 2 million homes and businesses were without electricity, and it took weeks to restore power. Schools were closed for up to two weeks—all fifty-nine of the schools in Osceola County were damaged.

Even after traveling half the length of the state to Orlando, the winds were still at hurricane speed. The damage estimate approached $15 billion.

10 SHIPWRECKS

The length of Florida's coastline is counted two ways. Going in a more or less straight line from Jacksonville down the east coast, looping around and up the west coast and over to Pensacola is about 1,300 miles. But if you count all of the inlets and bays, the total soars to almost 8,500 miles, second only to Alaska. The coast has been an attraction for smugglers, armies, pirates, developers and tourists for centuries.

THE *TRINITÉ*

The sinking of the French flagship *Trinité* in 1565 played a significant role in Florida history. It decided whether Florida would become a Spanish colony or a French colony.

In the 1560s, French Protestants—known as Huguenots—looked to the New World to create a colony where they could practice their religion freely. Catholic Spain was determined to prevent this. The French came first, establishing Fort Caroline near present-day Jacksonville in 1562. Jean Ribault was assigned to resupply the French colony, which was facing starvation. His seven ships carried weapons, livestock, five hundred soldiers and another five hundred seamen and colonists.

The king of Spain dispatched Pedro Menéndez with eleven ships and one thousand soldiers to end the French presence in Florida. The Menéndez fleet encountered violent storms, and Menéndez had only five ships when he landed on the Florida coast in September. To the north, the French divided their troops, leaving a handful to guard Fort Caroline, while the bulk of their troops sailed south to attack the Spanish. It was a foolish strategy. The surviving French soldiers washed ashore around Cape Canaveral and began marching north, planning to get back to Fort Caroline.

Menéndez sent a force to attack the nearly helpless Fort Caroline, a battle that lasted only a brief time. Some of the French escaped to a ship in the St. Johns River, but the others were slaughtered and the Spanish flag was raised. Menéndez then headed south, met the French at Matanzas Inlet and slaughtered nearly all of them, sparing those who professed to be Catholic. In Spanish, *matanzas* means "slaughter."

The site of Fort Caroline has never been found, and some researchers have placed it as far north as Georgia. In 2016, the wreck of the French ship *Trinité* was found by a treasure salvage company off Cape Canaveral. The question of ownership ended up in the courts. The salvage company claimed that the ship could not be identified definitively and was theirs. But France claimed that it was *La Trinité* and belonged to the French navy.

A U.S. court ruled that *La Trinité* belonged to France and could not be salvaged. The artifacts on the ship included a monument that was to be used to claim what the French thought would be French Florida, but instead it ended up at the bottom of the ocean.

ATOCHA AND *SANTA MARGARITA*

The mystery of the 1622 Spanish treasure fleet remains four hundred years later. While most of the ships have been found, three are still missing. The search goes on.

The Spanish Crown was fighting the Thirty Years' War and desperately needed cash. But five times between 1550 and 1733, the Spanish fleet failed to reach Spain, falling victim to storms that sent billions in gold and silver to the bottom.

In 1622, there were two Spanish treasure fleets that gathered in Havana and the New Spain fleet. The *Tierra Firme* fleet came from South America loaded with pearls, gold, emeralds and silver. The New Spain fleet was from Mexico with silver, gold and goods from the Orient such as silk and porcelain.

Most of the wealth was transferred to the more heavily armed *Tierra Firme* fleet, and the delay meant that the twenty-eight-vessel fleet did not leave Havana until the height of hurricane season. The ships were near the

Florida Keys when a storm struck, separating the fleet. Twenty of the ships managed to ride out the storm, but eight were forced onto reefs and sank.

The two most valuable ships were the *Atocha* and the *Santa Margarita*. The *Santa Margarita* was a large Spanish galleon with twenty-five cannons carrying the bulk of the Spanish coin—166,574 silver Spanish dollars, known as pieces of eight, along with more than 5,000 silver ingots and an untold quantity of smuggled gold and silver, brought aboard by crewmen and officials who wanted to avoid a tax that could run from 20 to 40 percent. The *Santa Margarita* was partly salvaged, but the Spanish could not find the *Atocha*, which remained a mystery for more than three centuries.

Mel Fisher attracted investors to search for the *Nuestra Señora de Atocha* beginning in 1969, a search that lasted for nearly seventeen years. In 1975, Fisher's son, Dirk; his wife, Angel; and a diver died when their boat sank while looking for the treasure. It was dangerous, difficult work, and success finally came in 1985. Fisher found $450 million in gold and silver. He called it the "*Atocha* Motherlode," and it included forty tons of gold and silver, emeralds and one thousand silver ingots.

Still, more than half of the ship's bounty is missing. The State of Florida claimed 25 percent of his find, but a seven-year court battle awarded the entire find to Fisher.

The wreck is forty miles off the coast of Key West. The Fisher family has created the Atocha Dive Adventure (melfisher.com), which gives divers a chance to look for treasure at the *Atocha* site. There is still lots of treasure at the site—gold and silver listed on the ship manifest that remains missing. The program lasts a week.

MAPLE LEAF

A key part of Abraham Lincoln's Civil War strategy was to blockade Southern ports to keep valuable cotton from going to mills in England and keep European goods—including guns and ammunition—from helping the South. The Confederate navy was small and no match for the Union navy. But Confederate secretary of the navy Stephen Mallory was inventive.

Mallory was born in the British West Indies, but his family settled in the port city of Key West in 1820. He was elected to the United States Senate in 1850 and left the Senate when Florida left the Union in 1861. Confederate president Jefferson Davis sought geographic balance for his cabinet and named Mallory to the navy post.

Mallory grew up with the sea—his widowed mother operated a boardinghouse for sailors, and he became a maritime lawyer. At the start of the war, Mallory sought to enlist pirates for the Confederacy, giving them permission to attack Union ships, but the strategy was not as effective as Mallory hoped.

But two of his other ideas were to have lasting effect. The first was his enthusiasm for ironclad ships. Rather than try the impossible—produce more ships than the Union—he thought that fewer ships with armor would be the answer. His first ship, the CSS *Virginia*, sank two Union ships and proved that ironclads could work. He could not build on that success, however, and other ironclad vessels met with varying degrees of failure. He was more successful with the introduction of mines. In 1862, the USS *Cairo* sank, the first victim of mines.

In Florida, Union troops took control of coastal areas, such as St. Augustine, early in the war, but the state remained an important breadbasket for the Confederate army, providing salt and beef. The St. Johns River was the key to the heart of Florida, and Mallory was determined to keep Union ships out of the interior.

Florida provided just fifteen thousand soldiers for the Confederate army but was a vital source for beef and salt. Saltworks were established along the coast. Salt was used in everything from curing beef to making boots.

Defense of the river became even more vital in 1864. Union soldiers were desperately needed farther north, and General Pierre Beauregard was ordered to abandon Camp Milton. He ordered torpedoes to be laid in the St. Johns, just two days before the *Maple Leaf* sailed up the river.

The large ship was used to transport soldiers during the war, but on this voyage from Palatka the ship had just three Confederate prisoners and a group of Union supporters who wanted to flee Florida. It carried four hundred tons of Union baggage. When the ship hit the mine, with its seventy pounds of gunpowder, four Union soldiers were killed—the first casualties of a mine.

The ship took just seven minutes to sink in twenty-four feet of water and came to rest in the thick mud on the bottom. The *Maple Leaf* was one of the larger transport ships, and even in twenty-four feet of water, the upper deck was deemed a threat to navigation by the government and removed in the 1880s. It was rediscovered in 1984, and divers removed nearly one thousand pounds of cargo, including shaving kits and belt buckles.

It is a National Historic Landmark. The *Maple Leaf* Museum (mandarinmuseum.net) is open on Saturday. It is located at 11964 Mandarin Road in Jacksonville.

URCA DE LIMA

By 1715, the Spanish learned that a single ship carrying valuable cargo was an open invitation to pirates lurking along the Florida coast. They had already found that the Gulf Stream ran along the Florida coast and then near the coast of the Carolinas turned east toward Europe. It provided something of a superhighway for ships heading from the New World to Spain.

The wealth of the New World financed the Spanish empire, and the government decided to combine its ships into a fleet to protect against pirates. The fleet system began around 1530. In 1715, ships from the Spanish territories assembled in Havana and departed in late July for Spain. In the Atlantic, a hurricane was gathering steam and reached what is now Vero Beach at the same time as the fleet on July 31, 1715.

The *Urca de Lima* sailed from Spain to gather wealth in Veracruz, Mexico, and then to Havana to join about a dozen other ships for the journey. The cargo included a large quantity of gold bullion and 14 million pesos of silver. The storm sank all but one of the ships, and some 1,500 sailors died. Only a few managed to survive in lifeboats.

Within a month, ships arrived from Havana and began searching for salvage. Those ships close to the Florida coast had their masts above the waterline, and the Spanish burned the tops to hide the location from pirates seeking sunken treasure. The search continued for three centuries, and most people assumed that all the treasure had been recovered. But in 2015, $4.5 million in gold coins from the 1715 shipwreck was found. Three hundred years later, coins still occasionally wash ashore.

The *Urca de Lima* is protected as a Florida Underwater Archaeological Preserve. It is open to public diving, and because it is so close to the shore, it has been popular. It is located about two hundred yards offshore near Pepper Beach Park near Fort Pierce.

SAN PEDRO

Despite the disaster of the 1715 Spanish fleet, the Spanish stuck with the system of sending ships in fleets to discourage pirates and privateers from other nations. And they stuck with the schedule, sailing during the summer at the start of the hurricane season.

In 1733, the fleet left Havana for Spain, with a stop in St. Augustine. There were twenty-one ships in all, enough to frighten even the most brazen pirate. As the ships approached the Florida Keys, the wind picked up, and Lieutenant General Rodrigo de Torres ordered the ships to turn back for Havana. The orders came too late. The storm drove the ships west, leaving them in ruins along the Keys, either sunk, swamped or scattered. Four ships were able to return to Havana, and one eventually made it to Spain.

A ship sailing into Havana reported the disaster, and rescue ships were sent out to seek survivors and the lost wealth. Because the ships were spread out over a wide area, the search for the lost gold and silver went on for years. As with the 1715 fleet, the Spanish burned the tops of the ships to hide the wrecks from pirates and posted ships to protect the sites.

The Spanish salvage operation was so successful that they found more gold and silver than was listed on the manifests on some ships. That was a result of smuggling minerals from the mines to Spain to avoid taxes. Everyone from ordinary seamen to officers managed to take some wealth back to Spain. Despite its efforts, Spain was unable to recover much of the treasure, and it remained on the bottom.

The *San Pedro*, one of the ships in this fleet, was rediscovered in the 1960s with thousands of silver coins on board. Today, it is a favorite of divers.

The remains of the sunken ship *San Pedro* have become a favorite spot for divers.

POTRERO DEL LLANO

The *Potrero del Llano* was one of scores of large, lumbering oil tankers that regularly sailed from Texas to the East Coast loaded with oil. The ship changed ownership several times before being purchased by an Italian firm. The ship traveled to Tampico, Mexico, in 1940. Italy had joined the Axis Powers in 1939, and one day after the Japanese attack on Pearl Harbor, Mexico seized the ship.

In May 1942, the newly renamed *Potrero del Llano* was sailing along the Florida coast carrying 6,132 tons of petroleum. The captain of German submarine *U-564* spotted the ship near Miami and fired, even though the ship displayed a Mexican flag and Mexico was not at war with Italy or Germany. Thirteen crewmen went down with the ship, but twenty-two crewmen were saved and taken to Miami. One of the survivors, Jose Reyes Sosa, survived a second attack just one month later.

Six days later, a second Mexican tanker sank, and two days later, Mexico declared war on the Axis nations. Two more Mexican tankers were sunk during the war by German submarines.

Hundreds of wrecks have been located off the Florida coast, but the exact location of the *Potrero del Llano* remains a mystery. The ship caught fire and the crew was rescued, but no one actually saw it sink. In 2011, a research vessel used a deep-water multibeam sonar to seek the remains but failed to find any sign of the ship. Experts doubt that the ship will ever be found.

SS COMMODORE

Few people have heard of the SS *Commodore* today, but it was once the most famous sunken ship in the United States. Its story produced a bestselling book by one of the nation's best-known writers.

The *Commodore* was a steamship operating out of Jacksonville in 1897 as war fever was sweeping the nation. The *Commodore* was one of dozens of ships running contraband from Jacksonville to Cuba, to the revolutionaries seeking to overthrow the Spanish. Jacksonville was the center of anti-revolution activity, and Spanish spies were active.

One of those seeking to go to Cuba was Stephen Crane, who shot to fame during the Civil War with his novel *The Red Badge of Courage*. Crane spent weeks in Jacksonville seeking a ship to take him to Cuba. The *Commodore* was hauling not only Crane but also forty bundles of rifles and more than 200,000 shells.

Two miles offshore, the ship struck a sandbar and had to wait for help. Once off the reef, the ship ran into foul weather. The pumps failed, and the passengers began bailing with buckets. They could not keep up with the rising water, and attempts to reach shore failed.

Thirteen miles from the coast, in the violent storm, the ship began to sink, and three lifeboats were lowered. Passengers and crew crammed into the three lifeboats, but Crane, the captain and several others were left standing on the deck; they found a small dinghy instead. As 1897 began, Crane was fighting for his life in the Atlantic.

The next morning, two lifeboats reached shore, but when the third lifeboat came ashore, it was empty. The Crane dinghy finally reached shore near Daytona Beach, but one of the crewmen drowned shortly before reaching land. It took Crane four days to reach Jacksonville, where he found that his rescue was front-page news. He wrote his story for a newspaper syndicate, and it was sold to newspapers around the country. He wrote a longer story for *Scribner's Magazine* and then a book, *The Open Boat*. Although he finally reached Cuba, the story of his ordeal in the boat drew far more attention.

Nearly a century later, the wreckage was found about twelve miles off the coast of Daytona Beach. Led by Don Serbousek, the Anchor Chasers Dive Club found rifles and bullets under sediment. The Lilian Place Heritage Center in Daytona Beach is where Crane spent the night after being saved. It was built in 1884 and is the oldest home on the beach side of Daytona Beach. It is open Wednesday through Monday in the afternoon (lilianplacehc.org). The Ponce de Leon Inlet Lighthouse (ponceinlet.org) is an excellent source of information about the *Commodore*, and Lead Docent John Mann has developed a following for his portrayal of the captain of the *Commodore*.

CITIES SERVICE EMPIRE

On December 8, 1941, the United States declared war on Japan, and three days later, Germany declared war on the United States. The first attacks came on Pearl Harbor, but the second wave of attacks took place in the Atlantic off the East Coast of the United States. The death toll reached five thousand—more than twice as many as were killed at Pearl Harbor—and nearly 20 percent of the oil tanker fleet was sunk.

As soon as war was declared, German submarines left for the United States. Their captains were surprised that the lights were still on in cities along the Florida coast. For the Germans, they provided the perfect backdrop for oil tankers heading for cities in the Northeast.

On February 22, World War II came to Florida. The *Republic* was passing Jupiter Island Lighthouse when it was struck by two torpedoes, destroying the engine room and killing three men instantly. The ship began listing, and the captain gave the order to abandon ship. The men boarded two lifeboats. One boat with twenty-two survivors on board rowed to shore; the other boat was picked up by another ship and taken to Port Everglades.

The *Republic* was passing Jupiter when it was attacked and sunk by a German U-boat.

When the survivors reached the shore, they found residents waiting to help them. It became a common occurrence for the months that the U-boats roamed at will. Sometimes crew members arrived in lifeboats, but often they were washed up. Some were covered with oil and some had serious burns; residents came down to care for them. The *Republic* drifted and sank the next day.

The U.S. Coast Guard was still responding to the *Republic* attack when a German U-boat fired six torpedoes at the *Cities Service Empire*, an oil tanker that was sailing near Vero Beach. The first four torpedoes missed their mark, but the final two struck the ship. Both hit the middle of the ship and set off a fire. The guards rushed for the guns on deck to fire back but were driven back by the flames. Within ten minutes, the order was given to abandon ship; the lifeboats had been consumed by the fire, so just two rafts were launched. Most of the men, fifty in all, leaped into the sea, but three men were left in the bow of the ship. The Coast Guard cutter USS *Vigilant* was nearby and rushed to help. The cutter nosed up to the *Empire*, and two of those on the bow were rescued; they were trying to rescue the third when the ship exploded and broke in two. Nineteen minutes after the first torpedo hit, the ship slipped beneath the water. The captain was on a life raft with some other men, but the current carried them back toward the fire. A wiper on the *Empire* watched from a lifeboat and said later, "I saw our captain on a life raft. He and some of the other men were on it and the current was sucking them into the burning oil around the tanker. I last saw the captain going into a sheet of orange flame. Some of the fellows said he screamed....Monroe Reynolds was with me for a while. He was screaming that he was going blind....Gus, the quartermaster, was with us. He had a piece of steel in his head and he said, 'I won't last long.' He didn't." Fourteen men were lost, and thirty-four survivors were picked up by another ship and taken to Fort Pierce.

The *Empire* sits in about 240 feet of water and is a favorite of divers. It rests about thirty miles east of Cape Canaveral, and divers traditionally use the ships at Port Canaveral for day trips to the site.

GULFAMERICA

As Nazi submarines struck ships along the East Coast, some cities instituted blackouts, but others did not. Jacksonville Beach, a small community south of Jacksonville, did not have a blackout. The *Gulfamerica*, a tanker loaded with more than 100,000 barrels of furnace oil, was heading north on April 10, 1942, when it sailed by Jacksonville Beach and was illuminated by the town's lights. The ship had been steaming in an evasive pattern but decided to stop. Minutes later, a torpedo struck the ship and set off a fire.

The captain gave the command to abandon ship and sent out distress signals. Then the captain of the submarine did something that surprised everyone. The U-boat surfaced to use its deck guns to complete its work, but the captain realized that the town was behind the ship and errant shots might strike civilians on the shore. The beach and its boardwalk were crowded, and there was a dance on the pier. The fire at sea brought many of them to the water's edge. The captain knew that many of them would be killed. He maneuvered his ship around the *Gulfamerica* so that shots could not hit the town. The U-boat began firing with its deck gun, sending a dozen shells into the engine room. The shooting caused confusion, and one of the lifeboats capsized.

The delay in moving his ship to avoid hitting the coast cost the German commander valuable time and allowed the destroyer USS *Dahlgren* to approach and open fire, damaging the submarine, which limped back to Europe. The initial blast killed five men, and fourteen more drowned. The ship took nearly a month to finally sink. The incident led Jacksonville Beach to institute a blackout, but it was months before it became mandatory along the coast. Half a century later, the captain of the sub visited Jacksonville and received a warm welcome.

The *Gulfamerica* sits in about sixty feet of water several miles off Jacksonville Beach. The ship has become one of the most magnificent reefs off the Florida coast. The location and beauty make it one of the state's most popular dive sites, especially for those from North Florida. There are regular dive trips from Jacksonville.

USS NARCISSUS

In 1863, the tugboat *Mary Cook* was built in East Albany, New York, and quickly purchased by the U.S. Navy. It was commissioned the USS *Narcissus* in early 1864 and sent to New Orleans. Under the command of Admiral David Farragut, the ship took part in a number of operations along the Gulf Coast.

The ship struck a mine and sank. A few days after Christmas, it was refloated and spent the rest of the war undergoing repairs in Pensacola. With the war over, the United States started to sell many of the ships, including the *Narcissus*. The *Narcissus* and the USS *Althea* were sent to New York for decommission and sale.

On January 4, 1866, the two ships encountered a storm off the coast of Tampa and decided to anchor and wait out the storm off the coast. The *Althea* headed to the northeast to anchor, while the *Narcissus* headed west. Even with the poor weather, the *Narcissus* was traveling at full speed when it hit a sandbar. The *Althea* was also briefly grounded but broke free.

Those on the *Althea* saw flares coming from the *Narcissus*. On the *Narcissus*, the boiler exploded, and as the crew of the *Althea* watched, the *Narcissus* broke up and sank with its entire crew—about two dozen men.

As dawn came, the wreck could be seen, and the beaches of Egmont Key were littered with the remains of the ship. The *Althea* spent two days looking for survivors but found none and headed for New York.

The remains of the ship came to rest in shallow water near Egmont Key, just outside Tampa Bay. A century and a half after the sinking, it became one of twelve Underwater Archaeological Preserve sites. The ship sits 2.75 miles northeast of Egmont Key in just fifteen feet of water. There are charter trips to the site. The ship is still owned by the U.S. Navy, and as it is a burial site for sailors, it has been preserved.

10 MOVIES

Filmmaking first began in Tampa and Key West in 1898. Film crews sent by Thomas Edison came to film the military activity in preparation for the attack on Cuba in the Spanish-American War. Their work was shown around the country at kinescope parlors and vaudeville houses. In Key West, Edison's men filmed the funerals for sailors killed in the explosion of the USS *Maine*. Florida had its chance to become the capital of moviemaking—the Hollywood of the world. But things went badly, and Florida's star turn lasted just a few years.

Thomas Edison not only created the movie industry, but in its early years he also controlled it with an iron hand. Edison made a deal with Eastman Kodak to control Eastman Kodak's movie film, which meant that anyone who wanted to make a movie had to use Edison's equipment and get the film from him. He used that power to decide how long a movie could be and the subject matter.

The first movies were made under Edison's watchful eye at the studio he built, a barn-like building nicknamed the "Black Maria." An ongoing problem was the weather. In the North, there was a shortage of daylight in the winter months and the skies were often overcast. Because of the need for light, indoor scenes often needed to be filmed outdoors, impossible when it was snowing.

In 1908, Edison's Kalem Studios came to Jacksonville, then the center of business in Florida. Within a month, the studio had finished its first film, *A Florida Feud: or, Love in the Everglades.* The brief film took advantage not only

Florida weather drew dozens of movie companies. In 1925, a movie company filmed in Coral Gables.

of the weather but also the scenery, including what one writer called the "real tropical scenery." It was a major hit, and other film companies noticed. Kalen dramatically increased its output, producing eighteen films running from fifteen to thirty minutes. The moviemakers took advantage not only of the jungles but also the beaches and downtown Jacksonville.

Within a few years, there were more than two dozen movie companies in Jacksonville, and Major J.E.T. Bowden was making plans for even more expansion. But the welcome was not universal. Many in the city objected to the presence of the movie companies for several reasons centering on their behavior. The "movie people" were known to drink—in a conservative, dry state—to fail to keep the Sabbath and to sometimes ask the citizens to help finance dubious moviemaking projects.

The filmmakers staged false bank robberies to draw large crowds while making their films, pulled fire alarms to film fire scenes and, in one case, arranged for 1,200 extras for a mob scene that turned into a real riot with substantial damage. In 1917, Bowden was voted out of office by a candidate running on an anti-movie platform.

Movie companies had begun the move to California by the end of 1917. One of those closing was Eagle Film City, which sold its abandoned studios to Richard Norman. Norman's idea was to make movies featuring African American actors for the African American audience. It was a bold idea in the 1920s. Filmmakers such as D.W. Griffith had cast African Americans in a negative light in films such as *Birth of a Nation*. Norman cast them as strong heroes in action movies and westerns. He produced eight feature films, including his greatest hit, *The Flying Ace*. Norman's undoing was talking pictures, which came in 1927. Norman, along with many other producers, could not afford the expensive transition to movies with sound. The situation was particularly precarious for Norman; most of the theaters catering to African American audiences could not afford to add sound systems, but those that did demanded that movies talk.

Although the other studios disappeared, somehow the buildings housing the Norman Studios remained in Jacksonville's Arlington neighborhood. For a time, his wife turned the studio into a dance studio. In the 1990s, the buildings were rediscovered, and an effort was launched to preserve them. The City of Jacksonville purchased the buildings, and private money was raised to rehabilitate them. The studio was placed in the National Register of Historic Places and designated a National Historic Landmark (normanstudios.org).

Jacksonville's Norman Studios made films for African American audiences.

Florida was the perfect setting for re-creating the jungles of Africa. This scene featured "Boy," the son of Tarzan and Jane.

While Jacksonville lost the movie business, South Florida began to attract filmmakers. In 1920, the industry's greatest director, D.W. Griffith, came to Fort Lauderdale to film *The Idol Dancer*. Advertisements for the film proclaimed that the film was "actually taken in the Southern Seas," but these Southern Seas were not in the Pacific Ocean, but rather off the southern United States.

The Great Depression came to Florida early following the two vicious hurricanes and the collapse of the land boom in 1928. Governor Doyle Carlton backed state efforts to lure the filmmakers back to Florida with tax incentives. In 1930, Florida's first talkie, *Hell Harbor*, was filmed in Tampa, a city chosen because it was supposed to look like Havana.

Tarzan movies were a staple of the silent era, and in the 1930s, they began to be made as talking pictures starring Johnny Weissmuller and Maureen O'Sullivan. Camera crews filmed in Silver Springs and Wakulla Springs, although both have taken on exaggerated importance. They were chosen because the producers thought they looked like the African jungle. Parts of a total of six Tarzan movies were filmed in Florida, but film shot for one movie was subsequently used in other movies.

The Tarzan movies stirred widespread interest in Silver Springs and touched off a stampede of tourists, who came by the thousands to ride in the glass-bottom boats.

There were thoughts that Florida might once again claim the "movie capital" title in the 1980s. Both Disney World and Universal Studios planned to combine theme parks with motion picture studios. Orlando offered low costs and great weather. Using the slogan "Hollywood weather without the Hollywood overhead," the state thought that anything was possible. The studios were built, but what had been billed as "Hollywood East" never materialized. Producers did not like the idea of making movies while tourists filed by, and the studios found that Canada offered more lucrative tax breaks. Plus, the stars remained in California, and the cost of transporting them back and forth often offset any gains in cost savings. Instead, Orlando became the "Infomercial Capital" of the nation, with thousands of films for industry and corporations.

CREATURE FROM THE BLACK LAGOON

Universal Studios practically invented the monster movie, unleashing Dracula, Frankenstein and the Wolfman on the world. The studio even combined its franchises, linking Abbott and Costello with Frankenstein and the Wolfman. There were still space monsters to film, but by the 1950s, the genre seemed to have run its course. A Universal executive heard the story of a monster lurking in the Amazon and thought it might be perfect. Although *Creature from the Black Lagoon* is forever linked to Florida, like many of what are considered "Florida movies," most of the film was shot in California, on the Universal lot.

But the key scenes of the movie that inspire the terror were filmed in Wakulla Springs, south of Tallahassee. The film was made in 3-D, and the underwater scenes are still considered some of the best underwater cinematography ever made. A local swimmer, Ricou Browning, was tapped to play the monster, and a young woman from Sebring, Ginger Stanley, appeared in most of the underwater scenes as the stand-in for star Julie Adams. (She was also the double for Esther Williams in *Jupiter's Darling* in 1955.) Adams had an ear infection and was unable to do many underwater scenes.

Actress Julie Adams was suffering from an ear infection during filming of *Creature from the Black Lagoon*, so a double took her place for underwater scenes.

The movie was a hit and led to the sequel, *Revenge of the Creature*. Browning and Stanley returned, but Julie Adams was replaced by Lori Nelson. Clint Eastwood made his motion picture debut in this one. Much of that movie was filmed at Marineland near St. Augustine, with scenes shot along the St. Johns River, in Silver Springs near Ocala and in Palatka's Rice Creek.

It was not as successful as the first movie, and the use of 3-D was fading fast by this point, but it did well enough for a third movie, *The Creature Walks Among Us*. It was filmed near Fort Myers on the Caloosahatchee River and at Wakulla Springs. In this one, the monster sheds some of his gills and begins wearing clothes. The only memorable thing is that the score was composed by a young Henry Mancini. The Creature movies had run their course.

Parts of the third film were made at Marineland, south of St. Augustine. Marineland was built with the idea that it would combine a tourist attraction with a movie studio. Wakulla Springs State Park is south of Tallahassee near the town of Crawfordville. The park features riverboat tours, snorkeling, swimming and deep springs. But alas, there are no scary creatures in the lagoons. (See floridastateparks.org/parks-and-trails/Edward-ball=Wakulla-springs-state-park.)

THE YEARLING

The Yearling won the Pulitzer Prize in 1939, but it took six years before it became a motion picture. Few films have run into the type of problems *The Yearling* encountered. Originally, Spencer Tracy was to star in the movie, but soon after he arrived in Florida in 1941, he found the heat and bugs unbearable and left. Production was halted for four years. The second time around, Gregory Peck was the star. Metro-Goldwyn-Mayer purchased the film rights and agreed with author Marjorie Kinnan Rawlings that much of the movie should be filmed in the area near her Florida home. Rawlings wrote the book in her farmhouse in an area known as "Big Scrub."

Peck, the star of the movie (although some people would think the fawn was the star), said, "Here was the scrub country. Not many people lived here then, just a few pioneers. I found myself a wonderful wife and a little village nearby." Not that much has changed; Florida has become the third-most populous state, but the area around the Rawlings home is still lightly populated.

Much of the movie was filmed in Ocala National Forest in a cabin purchased by the studio and moved to the forest. Rawlings was hired as a technical adviser but only came to the film site once or twice. One time she claimed to watch a scene where dogs chase a bear. But Rawlings said the dogs they brought in were "city dogs…and the old bear just looked up and he knew they were damn city dogs." The bear ended up chasing the dogs. Rawlings herself went out and rounded up the dogs that were used in the movie. They chased the bear into a river, and the bear swam away and was never seen again.

The Yearling was filmed at the Juniper Prairie Wilderness in the Ocala National Forest. It is easy to get to, running along State Road 40. It has no roads and no vehicles are allowed. It is perfect for backpacking, hiking or paddling. You must bring your own drinking water. Canoe rentals are available. (See fs.usda.gov/recarea/Ocala.)

THE COCOANUTS

The Cocoanuts was filmed in New York's Astoria Studios but is set in Florida and is a comedic take on the Florida land boom of the 1920s. The entire movie has very little in the way of plot but is designed to give the Marx Brothers a chance to use their gags. The movie takes place in the Hotel de Cocoanut and centers on land fraud and theft—two prominent themes in 1920s Florida. One of the classic lines comes when Groucho is working as an auctioneer peddling worthless Florida land. He tells the potential buyers, "You can have any kind of home you want to; you can even get stucco! Oh, how you can get stuck-oh!" He uses his brother Chico to inflate the land price by calling out false bids, a tactic used in 1920s Florida. Chico keeps driving up the price, even bidding against himself. Most of the songs in the movie were written by Irving Berlin, including "Florida by the Sea":

In the lovely land of Florida
Sunny Florida by the sea

All the sunshine in America
Is in Florida you'll agree

When they're freezing up north
Sneezing up north
Always it's July the Fourth

THUNDERBALL

Ian Fleming clearly liked Florida, and the people who turned his James Bond novels into movies followed suit. Fleming set part of his 1954 novel in St. Petersburg. In the book, the hunt is on for pirate treasure that has been turning up in Florida. Bond meets his nemesis there on the aptly named Treasure Island, which is next to St. Petersburg. Bond is not impressed with the city—"For heaven's sake, what sort of place are we going to?" In the book, Fleming described the city this way: "When the bank clerk or the post-office workers or the railroad conductor reaches sixty, he collects his pension or his annuity and goes to St. Petersburg to get a few years sunshine before he dies." But the city did not make it into the movie.

In *Goldfinger*, Fleming set his opening in Miami, where Bond encounters Goldfinger. In the movie, there are scenes of the magnificent Fontainebleau Hotel, but it is a filmmaker's trick. Goldfinger and Bond are sitting in a studio in London, while film of the hotel is in the background.

Some stock footage of a rocket launch was used in the film *You Only Live Twice*. In *Moonraker*, Florida is used extensively, but not as Florida. Cape Kennedy is supposed to represent a site in California, the St. Lucie River near Jupiter is supposed to be the Amazon and Silver Springs is the site for an underwater scene representing a foreign body of water.

License to Kill used Florida extensively, starting in Key West and including the Overseas Bridge and the Key West Airport. In the 2006 remake of *Casino Royale*, Daniel Craig appears in a Miami museum and at Miami International Airport, but it is another trick—the film was shot in Prague.

Author Ian Fleming used Florida as a backdrop for some of his James Bond books, but only one, *Thunderball*, had extensive filming in Florida. This is one of the underwater scenes.

It is *Thunderball* that relies on Florida the most. The extensive underwater scenes were filmed in Silver Springs. Amazingly, the filming was choreographed by Ricou Browning, who had played the creature in the *Creature from the Black Lagoon* a decade earlier.

COCOON

Ian Fleming may have been dismissive of St. Petersburg, but for director Ron Howard, it was perfect. Howard planned a movie dealing with extraterrestrials and their effect on the elderly. The aliens have a pool that rejuvenates the elderly. Don Ameche won an Academy Award for his role as a senior citizen, and Wilford Brimley and Hume Cronyn costarred. It was filmed in 1984 and featured as extras local citizens who were paid twelve dollars per day. The movie won two Academy Awards, one for Don Ameche as Best Supporting Actor and for Best Visual Effects. The movie was a huge hit and led to a sequel that was filmed in Miami. It did not include Howard as director and was not nearly as successful. Scenes throughout St. Petersburg were used, including the city shuffleboard courts, the dolphin tanks at Busch Gardens in nearby Tampa and homes on Snell Isle.

WHERE THE BOYS ARE

Few movies have had the ongoing economic impact on Florida as *Where the Boys Are*. It touched off the annual pilgrimage of students on Spring Break to beach destinations from Fort Lauderdale to Panama City.

The movie was far from a classic when it was filmed in 1960. It takes place in Fort Lauderdale, although almost all the filming was done in Hollywood. The film shows a far different Fort Lauderdale than today. Many areas where high-rise buildings stand today were empty lots in 1960s.

The boys began coming in the 1930s, when an Olympic-size pool was built in Fort Lauderdale, drawing swimming teams from around the country. After World War II, the number of students began to increase. The 1958 novel *Where the Boys Are* increased the turnout, and the 1960s movie and hit song by Connie Francis started a stampede. After the movie was released, attendance soared to 50,000 and eventually reached 350,000 in a single season.

Fort Lauderdale was booming, and high-end hotels and condos were going up everywhere. Spring Break brought in money but did little for the city's image. By the mid-1980s, the city was discouraging Spring Break, and students began heading to Daytona Beach, where MTV helped drive up attendance. But officials in Daytona Beach also grew tired of the influx and the damage and underage drinking it brought. The students headed to Panama City but gradually turned to cruises to places such as Mexico or even trips to Europe.

Scenes for the movie include the Elbo Room at 241 South Fort Lauderdale Beach Boulevard. In the movie, Connie Francis and Paula Prentiss, short on cash, turn hot water, crackers and ketchup into lunch. Scenes were also shot at the Wreck Bar at what is now the B Ocean Hotel. It features a nightly mermaid show. There is even a burlesque mermaid show. It is located at 1140 Seabreeze Boulevard.

The movie celebrated its sixtieth anniversary, and officials in Fort Lauderdale credit the movie with starting the boom that turned the sleepy beach town into a major city.

APOLLO 13

For many Americans, space flights had become old news by 1970. Just a year earlier, there had been the historic first landing on the moon, followed by another and then Apollo 13. Instead of being a routine trip,

Apollo 13 turned into the most memorable Apollo flight after the initial moon landing.

From the start, the mission was troubled. There were changes in the crew, and what was to have been the Apollo 14 crew became the Apollo 13 crew. One of the members of the new crew came down with the measles and was replaced. After the launch, a second stage engine cut off prematurely, but it did not seem to harm the mission.

When the three held a live news conference from space, interest had decreased to the point that the networks declined to carry it. Then a liquid oxygen tank exploded and another began to leak. The moon landing was aborted, and the lunar module became the crew's rescue vehicle. NASA had to come up with a way of getting them home.

They managed to return safely, but Jim Lovell never walked on the moon. He wrote a book about the mission that became the basis for the movie, which starred Tom Hanks as Lovell. It won two Academy Awards of the nine for which it was nominated.

Much of the movie was filmed in Hollywood, including a motel scene in the "Florida" motel. The fifty-two-story Vehicle Assembly Building at Cape Kennedy was used in the filming, but the Saturn rocket was Hollywood trickery.

COOL HAND LUKE

When he wrote *Cool Hand Luke*, author Donn Pearce knew his subject well. Pearce spent time on the Florida chain gang and heard stories about Luke Jackson. In 1949, Pearce was arrested for burglary and sentenced to a prison camp in Tavares. That is where Pearce got the inspiration to write his novel and the screenplay with the classic line, "What we've got here is failure to communicate." Pearce described the camp as a "chamber of horrors." Prisoners on the chain gang worked from morning to night and were often beaten.

Originally, Telly Savalas was to be the star, but he was in Europe, and the producers would not wait. Paul Newman got the part instead.

The movie is set in Florida, but it was not filmed there. The producers sent photographers to Tavares to take pictures of the prison camp and measure the buildings. A duplicate was built in California.

The movie includes a scene based on a real tragic event. Luther Catrett was a prisoner at Tavares Prison Camp in 1949 along with Pearce. Catrett was sentenced to three years for a robbery but escaped from the road gang along with another prisoner. Guards organized a hunt and that night found the two inside the church. Catrett was holding what appeared to be an organ stool. A guard claimed that he was about to throw the stool, and he shot and killed Catrett. In the movie, Luke is killed after escaping to a church.

The prison is gone, and the chain gangs are no more.

One of the best-known scenes was filmed in Florida, although Paul Newman was not in it. The scene where prison guards and bloodhounds are chasing Luke was filmed near Jacksonville, but Newman was in Hollywood. A stunt double was actually being chased. The dogs were provided by the Florida Department of Corrections.

KEY LARGO

This was the fourth and final film pairing Humphrey Bogart with his wife, Lauren Bacall—a fifth movie was planned, but he died before it was made. Although called *Key Largo*, nearly the entire movie was filmed in Hollywood. The head of Warner Bros., Jack Warner, did not trust director John Huston with location shooting. Huston had spent a fortune filming *The Treasure of the Sierra Madre* on location, and Warner did not want him to leave town.

In the movie, gangster Johnny Rocco, played by Edward G. Robinson, has taken over the island and a lot more. He tells Humphrey Bogart, "Let me tell you about Florida politicians. I make them. I make them out of whole cloth, just like a tailor makes a suit."

The movie only has one shot of Key Largo, the opening sequence showing the Caribbean Club—where the movie is supposed to take place. Nevertheless, the Caribbean Club has become known as "where the famous movie *Key Largo* was filmed."

The Caribbean Club was one of the last hurrahs of Carl Fisher, who had made a fortune in the automobile industry, built the racetrack at Indianapolis and filled in a mangrove swamp to create Miami Beach. He eventually went broke, and the Caribbean Club passed from his control. When it opened in 1938—a year before Fisher's death—it was a fishing camp. Several fires have changed it over the years, but it still stands and is still a tourist attraction.

The movie made Key Largo famous. It was a hit—earning an Academy Award for actress Claire Trevor—and people who had never heard of the uppermost key began discovering it.

FOLLOW THAT DREAM

Elvis Presley movies followed a predictable formula—a light plot and lots of songs—and *Follow that Dream* followed that script. It was filmed in Yankeetown, Tampa, Inverness and Ocala. The courthouse and the fishing camp scenes were filmed in Yankeetown, a town on the Gulf of Mexico west of Ocala. Presley stayed at the Port Paradise Hotel in Crystal River during the filming. In Ocala, he filmed the bank scene, which turned into an ordeal. The microphones picked up the bank's air conditioning motor, and it had to be turned off. It became unbearably hot in the bank, and when Elvis stepped outside for a breath of fresh air, he found a huge crowd gathering. He began to twist his hips as if he was singing "Hound Dog," and the crowd went wild.

For Elvis, it was a triumphant return to Florida. He first came in 1955, touring with big-name acts such as country singer Hank Snow and Andy Griffith. Elvis was far down on the bill—number eight with Snow's show. A year later, after the release of "Hound Dog," he was one of the most famous performers in the world.

Elvis stayed at the Port Hotel in Crystal River, generally called the Port Paradise Hotel. It is still a major drawing card. In Ocala, he filmed the bank scene at the former Commercial Bank and Trust Company on State Road 40. The courthouse scene was filmed in Inverness, and the fishing camp scene was filmed at Yankeetown.

22 U.S. PRESIDENTS

GEORGE WASHINGTON

You could forgive George Washington for disliking Florida. It caused him nothing but trouble. The troubles began at the start of the American Revolution, when East and West Florida remained loyal to King George III. As the Revolution dragged on, Florida became a haven for Tories fleeing the thirteen colonies. The fighting and confusion of war allowed slaves to escape the plantations of Georgia and the Carolinas and find refuge and British protection in Florida. The British army used the fort in St. Augustine to hold rebel leaders. Three signers of the Declaration of Independence were held in the fort: Arthur Middleton, Edward Rutledge and Thomas Heyward Jr. The Patriots tried to capture St. Augustine but were unsuccessful.

As part of the peace treaty ending the Revolution, the British returned Florida to the Spanish, but that did not end Washington's problems. The Spain that retook control of Florida was no longer the mighty nation it had been in the 1500s and 1600s. Spain could not adequately police Florida, and it became a mecca for runaway slaves, marauding Indians and even pirates. Washington argued with Spanish leaders over borders and spent nearly eight years negotiating a treaty with Spain.

THOMAS JEFFERSON

Even before becoming president, Thomas Jefferson was troubled by Florida. He was secretary of state under Washington when problems with Florida arose. He worried that somehow Britain would reacquire Florida and pose a threat to the new nation. "I am…deeply impressed with the magnitude of the dangers which will attend our government if Louisiana and Florida be added to the British Empire," he wrote Washington.

Jefferson's plan to add Florida to the United States involved encouraging Americans to move to Florida. He wrote to Washington, "I wish a hundred thousand of our inhabitants would accept the invitation"; he predicted that Florida would pass "naturally" if enough Americans moved there.

As president, he pulled off one of the greatest land deals in history, purchasing the Louisiana Territory from France. He dispatched James Monroe to Paris to purchase New Orleans and East and West Florida. Instead, Monroe came back with the Louisiana Territory, with the original goal forgotten. At first, Jefferson tried a bluff, claiming that West Florida had been part of the deal and offering Spain $2 million for East Florida. Spain rebuffed the claim and the money.

JAMES MADISON

When James Madison moved into the White House, West Florida was what one historian called the Wild West. Technically, Spain owned the territory, but no one was truly in control. American settlers tried to capture West Florida, apparently with the secret support of the United States. In 1810, the rebels seized the Spanish fort at Baton Rouge and proclaimed a republic. Madison moved to annex the land for the United States and divided the territory into parts of Louisiana, Alabama and Mississippi. Spain held Mobile until the War of 1812, when it was captured by American troops over the objections of the Spanish.

JAMES MONROE

It took James Monroe nearly two decades to win his prize. He began trying to acquire Florida in the early 1800s and completed the deal in 1819. By 1818, the United States acquired West Florida and set its sights on the rest of the

Spanish colony. Monroe sent General Andrew Jackson to stop Indian attacks on the United States from Florida. He was supposed to go *to* the border but instead invaded Florida, executed two British citizens and captured the Spanish governor at Pensacola. Monroe condemned the attack, although he may have secretly supported it. But Spain realized that it could no longer control Florida and opened negotiations to sell it. Secretary of State John Quincy Adams negotiated a treaty giving the United States all of Florida in exchange for paying up to $5 million to settle claims against Spain.

ANDREW JACKSON

Florida loved Andrew Jackson, naming its largest city and a county after him. But the love was hardly returned. Jackson came to Florida three times. He came in 1814 to fight the British during the War of 1812. He battled the British, and their allies the Spanish and the Creek Indians, for control of the city of Pensacola. Jackson won the only battle fought on Spanish soil. He returned during the First Seminole War (1816–19) to fight marauding Seminoles and executed two British merchants and captured the governor of Spanish Pensacola. When Florida became part of the United States, he was named the first territorial governor. His term lasted just a few unhappy months, with Jackson causing a series of problems. He quit and moved back to his plantation in Tennessee even before a replacement could be appointed.

His election as president in 1828 put the legendary Indian hater in the White House. He pushed through the Indian Removal Act, which required moving the Indians from Georgia and Florida to Arkansas. Jackson told the Indians, "I have then directed the Commanding officer to remove you by force." It touched off the Second Seminole War.

JOHN TYLER

John Tyler was elected as vice president on the Whig ticket in 1840 but found himself in the White House when William Henry Harrison died after just one month in office. He made it clear that he would not follow the Whig platform. He was a southern Democrat and strongly proslavery. There was a growing struggle between the slave and free slaves as the South sought to hold on to power in Washington. Tyler wanted as many slave states as possible in the Union to give the South greater power in Congress.

Tyler was never a serious candidate for reelection in 1844, but he was anxious to do one last favor for the slave South: days before his term ended, he signed legislation admitting Florida as a state. It was not without controversy—Florida wanted to come into the Union as two states, East Florida and West Florida, but agreed to come in as one state rather than having to wait.

ZACHARY TAYLOR

Along with Andrew Jackson, Zachary Taylor enhanced his military reputation in Florida. He came to Florida to try to do what other generals had failed to do. The army had only four major generals, and Edmund Gaines (namesake of Gainesville) and Winfield Scott tried and failed to suppress the Seminoles. A third, Major General Thomas Jesup (namesake of Lake Jesup), served in the Second Seminole War and had success in pushing the Seminoles south. Taylor was called to lead one column, and on Christmas Day, he fought the Indians near Lake Okeechobee. Although the battle was anything but a victory for Taylor, the nation needed a hero, and Taylor fit the bill. Jesup gave up his fight with the Indians, and Taylor took his place. Taylor was able to reduce the violence, but he realized that the war could not be won and asked for a transfer. Despite failing to defeat the Indians, he was famous and given command of troops in the war with Mexico. It propelled him into the White House in 1849.

ABRAHAM LINCOLN

The 1860 election of Abraham Lincoln led the southern states to leave the Union. South Carolina went first, and Florida quickly followed. Lincoln thought that if war came, it would start in Pensacola. Lincoln wanted to abandon Fort Sumter, which was impossible to defend, and reinforce Fort Pickens.

Confederate forces began to gather in Pensacola, and before Lincoln was sworn in, there were more than one thousand present, with four thousand more on the way. But Lincoln changed his mind and decided to resupply Fort Sumter. On April 12, the Confederates opened fire in Charleston. Two days later, fighting erupted in Pensacola, but the Union navy defeated the Confederates. Fort Pickens remained in Union hands throughout the war.

Florida's major contribution to the Confederacy was as a breadbasket, furnishing crops and cattle to feed the troops. But there was one major battle—one brought on by Lincoln. In 1864, Lincoln was worried that he would lose the election and began considering ways to help his chances. He thought that if he could somehow get Florida back into the Union, it would give him three more electoral votes. He dispatched troops, but the Union troops were soundly routed at the Battle of Olustee. It ended Lincoln's plan, and Tallahassee was the only Confederate capital east of the Mississippi that Union troops did not capture.

RUTHERFORD B. HAYES

On election night 1876, it appeared that Democrat Samuel Tilden was headed for victory. He had 184 electoral votes, just one short of a majority, and he led the popular vote by a wide margin. There were three states not accounted for, including Florida.

But the Republicans were not about to surrender the White House, and they challenged the results in Florida, South Carolina and Louisiana. Tilden was ahead in Florida, but by just ninety-one votes. Both parties sent operatives into Florida to try to steal the election. Bribes were offered, government jobs promised and political pressure used. The Republicans were more effective, and the three states went to the Republicans.

Behind the Hayes victory was a promise that the Republicans would withdraw federal troops from the South, thus ending Reconstruction. Hayes kept his bargain, and the former slaves began to lose the few rights they had gained.

CHESTER A. ARTHUR

Florida became a U.S. territory in 1821, but it took more than sixty years for a president to visit the state. Chester Arthur became president when James A. Garfield was assassinated in 1881. In 1883, Arthur came to Florida for politics and a vacation. His health was poor, but there was still speculation that he might be a candidate in 1884. He would need Florida's Republican delegates to help win re-nomination. Plus, he suffered from several ailments and needed a break from Washington. He came on a government mail train and switched to a steamboat in Jacksonville for the trip up the St. Johns River to Sanford and then on to Kissimmee by train. He went fishing in

Reedy Creek, which became famous eighty years later when Walt Disney chose the site for the home of Disney World.

Arthur returned to Washington with a healthy tan, but his heath was still poor. The trip brought tremendous publicity to Florida and helped make it a popular tourist destination.

GROVER CLEVELAND

By the late 1880s, Florida officials had realized that tourism could be a huge industry and bring the wealthy and their money to the state. Florida realized that it would need to attract visitors as other states were doing. State officials decided an exposition would bring national attention, and the presence of the president of the United States would guarantee front-page coverage. Cleveland accepted the invitation to attend the 1888 exposition—he was up for reelection—and brought his wife of two years, Frances.

The couple stayed at Jacksonville's finest hotel, the St. James, which was the first hotel in the state to have electricity. The *New York Times* called the visit the "greatest event in the history of Jacksonville." Cleveland traveled on to Titusville, Sanford, Rockledge and Winter Park.

The positive publicity about the wonders of Jacksonville ended abruptly four months later when yellow fever swept the city, killing nearly four thousand people.

President Grover Cleveland and his wife, Frances, stayed at a hotel in Rockledge.

WILLIAM McKINLEY

William McKinley launched the war in Cuba in 1898, which brought Florida thousands of soldiers and tremendous publicity. When war came, Floridians worried that Spain might attack the state. The government agreed to station soldiers around the coast. The biggest boon came in Tampa, which became the headquarters for troops departing for Cuba.

In 1899, McKinley came to Florida to campaign. He frequently visited Thomasville, Georgia, close to the Florida border. McKinley knew that he could not carry Florida when he ran for reelection in 1900, but Republicans in the state would play a role in selecting the nominee. McKinley crossed over into Monticello. From there, he went to Tallahassee, where the city was decked out in flags and bunting, and a parade was held in McKinley's honor. Although African Americans had few rights in Florida, they made up the bulk of the Republican Party. After an appearance at the capitol, he went to Florida A&M College, which had been established for African Americans a decade earlier. He declined to make a speech and stayed in the city for just a few hours before returning to Thomasville.

When President William McKinley visited Tallahassee, a man on a bull led the procession during a parade.

THEODORE ROOSEVELT

Theodore Roosevelt was assistant secretary of the navy when the Spanish-American War began, but within a few months he was one of the best-known men in the nation. He quit his post and formed a regiment known as the Rough Riders. He brought his men to Tampa, the embarkation spot for troops heading to Cuba. His unit was not supposed to sail, but he forced his way onto a transport ship and sailed for Cuba and fame. His actions on San Juan Hill propelled him to the vice presidency in 1900 and the White House one year later.

While Roosevelt was making his name as a military hero, Paul Kroegel was facing his own battle. Kroegel lived in Sebastian, and from his home

Teddy Roosevelt, *far right*, brought his Rough Riders to Tampa, which was the headquarters for the army in the Spanish-American War.

he could see Pelican Island and its thousands of magnificent birds. Their feathers were used for ladies' hats and literally worth their weight in gold. Kroegel began standing guard on the island, keeping the hunters away. His efforts and those of others led the legislature to pass laws to protect the birds. The Florida Audubon Society hired four men to patrol the island, but two were killed by hunters.

Two of Kroegel's friends knew Roosevelt and told him of the situation on Pelican Island. Roosevelt was moved and signed an executive order making the island the first federal bird reservation. Roosevelt went on to establish fifty-five bird reservations and create the Ocala National Forest, the oldest national forest east of the Mississippi River.

WARREN G. HARDING

Warren G. Harding loved Florida and began coming to the state well before his presidency. His father-in-law had a home in Daytona Beach, and he had friends on Merritt Island. After winning the presidency, he came to Florida to fish off Titusville and play poker and golf in Miami Beach. Miami Beach

Warren G. Harding was a frequent visitor to Florida. When he played golf in Miami Beach, the resort owner wanted to guarantee maximum publicity and purchased an elephant to serve as Harding's caddy.

developer Carl Fisher wanted to gather maximum publicity, so he purchased an elephant named Rosie to act as Harding's caddy.

Circus showman John Ringling approached Harding with an idea to build a winter White House on Bird Key. He suggested that a mansion he owned would be perfect. Harding liked the idea and agreed to visit Sarasota and inspect nearby Bird Key. But first, Harding planned a trip to Alaska and the West Coast. He died in San Francisco, and that ended the dream of a winter White House. In 1959, the mansion was torn down to make room for development.

CALVIN COOLIDGE

Calvin Coolidge loved Florida and came here as vice president and as president, as well as after his term ended. In 1929, as his term was ending, he came to Lake Wales to dedicate the beautiful Bok Tower.

To celebrate the end of his term, he returned to Florida for a monthlong vacation at the Lakeside Inn in Mount Dora. The structure—which still stands and remains a favorite getaway—was built in 1883. You can spend the night in the Calvin Coolidge suite, sleeping under a portrait of Silent Cal.

His vacation included a visit to Sanford to receive fresh fruit and to Winter Park, where hundreds of people welcomed him.

Calvin Coolidge came to Florida many times during and after his presidency. He received citrus from a delegation on one of those trips.

HERBERT HOOVER

In the 1928 election, Herbert Hoover became the first Republican to win Florida since Reconstruction. The economy was booming, although Florida's economy was already suffering as a result of deadly hurricanes, a land boom gone bust and bank failures. As the rest of the nation was plunged into depression, Hoover's popularity fell. After receiving 60 percent of the Florida vote in 1928, he received just 25 percent in 1932.

Hoover loved Florida and came often for the outdoor activities. He went camping with Henry Ford, Thomas Edison and Harvey Firestone, but the main attraction was fishing. For a decade, he held the state record for catching the largest bonefish. It was easy to spot Hoover, not only because he president, but because even while fishing he kept his tie and jacket on.

Hoover had made his fortune in building dams around the world, and friends said that during fishing trips he would put his pole down and build

Herbert Hoover came to Florida to fish and see old friends such as J.C. Penney. For years, he held the state record for catching the largest bonefish.

small dams from the rocks on the riverbank. He often went to Useppa Island off the Southwest Florida coast, joining author Zane Grey and others. In Miami, he stayed at the home of his friend J.C. Penney on an island between Miami and Miami Beach.

The hurricanes of 1926 and 1928 caused an unknown number of deaths and widespread flooding. Hoover, the dam builder, took a private interest in the situation, inspecting Lake Okeechobee personally and supporting the building of a dike. The dike was finished after he left the White House, and in 1961, an elderly Hoover attended the dedication of the Herbert Hoover Dike.

FRANKLIN ROOSEVELT

Roosevelt had a long history in Florida. After poliomyelitis left him partially paralyzed in 1921, Roosevelt was convinced that he could regain the use of his legs if he exercised. He purchased a yacht in Fort Lauderdale and began swimming in the waters along the Florida coast. Eventually, he

Franklin Roosevelt used his leg braces to stand when he arrived in Jacksonville during World War II.

A bullet intended for president-elect Franklin Roosevelt struck Chicago mayor Anton Cermak instead. Cermak later died at a Miami hospital.

realized that his condition would not improve, and he put the yacht up for sale. Before it could be sold, a hurricane drove the boat up the river and wrecked it on the shore. He continued to come to Florida, utilizing the yachts of friends.

After winning the presidency in 1932, Roosevelt came to Florida for a vacation aboard a yacht owned by Vincent Astor. There was pressure on Roosevelt to make a political appearance, and he agreed to make a few remarks at Bayfront Park in downtown Miami before leaving for New York. The plan was for him to remain in his convertible, and his speech was one of his shortest ever—just 132 words. Standing next to his car was Chicago mayor Anton Cermak, who happened to be in town. As Roosevelt spoke, Giuseppe Zangara, a mentally troubled man, approached, stepped on a chair, pulled out the eight-dollar pistol he had purchased and began firing. A woman nearby grabbed his arm as he fired, perhaps saving Roosevelt's life, but one of the wild shots struck Cermak, mortally wounding him. Other shots struck four other people. His limousine began to leave, but Roosevelt ordered the car stopped and helped pull Cermak into the back seat. The limousine drove Cermak to the hospital, where he died two days after Roosevelt's inauguration. Zangara was executed five weeks after the shooting.

HARRY S TRUMAN

For Harry Truman, a 1946 trip to Bermuda was a disaster. He became seasick and came down with a cold that seemed to go on for weeks. When he returned to Washington, he told Admiral Chester Nimitz about his terrible vacation. Nimitz told Truman about Key West and suggested it as a vacation spot. For Truman, it was a perfect solution. He was not a wealthy man, and the navy would provide a perfect spot for a vacation without charge.

In all, Truman spent more than six months of his administration in Florida and proclaimed Key West as his second-favorite place on Earth—behind only his hometown of Independence, Missouri.

As president, Truman made a decision that transformed a sleepy area of the Florida coast, turning it into the Space Coast. At the end of World War II, the military was operating a missile-testing range in White Sands, New Mexico, and encountering failure after failure. The erratic course of the rockets worried people living in the area, and when one hit Juarez, Mexico, it confirmed everyone's worst fears.

President Harry Truman fell in love with Key West and spent a total of six months on the island during his eight years in office.

After John Glenn's trip into space, Cocoa staged a parade for the astronaut. Vice President Lyndon Johnson sits on the right side of the car, while Glenn's wife, Annie, sits on the convertible top.

An alternative site in California was chosen but was also rejected. Florida finished third in the selection process but soon moved up to number one. On May 11, 1949, Truman signed legislation establishing the Long-Range Proving Ground at Cape Canaveral. The government already had large landholdings, including Patrick Air Force Base and the Naval Air Station Banana River. More land was added, and America's space program was underway.

Truman also helped preserve Florida's future in 1947 when he dedicated the Everglades National Park, which protected more than two thousand square miles. It provided protection for the priceless wetlands and wilflife from the threat of development.

JOHN F. KENNEDY

The Kennedy family came to Palm Beach in the 1930s when Joseph P. Kennedy purchased a home in Palm Beach, the new playground for the wealthy. John Kennedy came to Palm Beach as a teenager but did not spend as much time there as his younger siblings. First there was college, then military service and Palm Beach was largely forgotten. Childhood ailments, aggravated by his military service, led to a series of surgeries requiring long periods of recuperation. That was what brought him to Palm Beach and a new appreciation of the home. In 1954, he spent a long period at the home after back surgery—on and off for eight months. While recuperating, he worked on an idea he had for a book about courageous senators. It became *Profiles in Courage*. He had substantial help from his aide, Theodore Sorensen. After his presidential victory in 1960, he flew to Palm Beach to rest and choose his cabinet.

An almost forgotten episode in Palm Beach could have changed the course of history. At the time, the story of Richard Pavlick was little noted because of the collision of two planes over New York, which killed 128 people on the planes and 6 on the ground in Brooklyn. Pavlick had mental problems and was known to the Secret Service for sending threatening letters to previous

Four days before his death, John Kennedy campaigned in Miami and Tampa with Senator George Smathers.

presidents. He drove to Palm Beach with a car loaded with dynamite. His plan was to drive his car into Kennedy's car and set off an explosion. He saw Kennedy with Jacqueline and changed his mind—he did not want to kill her, just the president-elect.

Pavlick drove from the Kennedy home to St. Edwards Catholic Church with a new plan to kill Kennedy. A Secret Service agent saw the disheveled man among the well-dressed parishioners and watched as he walked down the center aisle toward Kennedy's pew. An agent approached, took Pavlick's elbow, pulled him back and led him out the door. Pavlick drove off, but agents alerted Palm Beach police, who found Pavlick's 1950 Buick containing ten sticks of dynamite and a detonation device. Pavlick was committed to a mental hospital.

Kennedy spent the last weekend of his life in Florida. He was a frequent visitor to Palm Beach during his presidency, and he flew to Palm Beach and then to Cape Canaveral to inspect progress on the space program. He made appearances in Miami and Tampa and then left Florida for the final time.

RICHARD NIXON

In 1950, Richard Nixon won a Senate seat in California and returned to his home in chilly Washington. At the Capitol, he ran into his good friend, George Smathers of Florida, who had also just been elected to the Senate. Nixon said he wanted to get away to warm weather for a break; the flight to California was lengthy, and once he arrived, everyone wanted to meet with him. Smathers had the solution: a flight to sunny Miami. He offered to have a friend meet Nixon in Key Biscayne and show him around. The friend was Bebe Rebozo, who became one of Nixon's closest friends.

Nixon became a regular visitor to Key Biscayne and flew to Palm Beach to meet with Kennedy after losing the 1960 election.

After winning the presidency in 1968, he again turned to his good friend George Smathers and asked him for a major favor. Would Smathers sell him his Key Biscayne home to use as a Florida White House? The homes on Key Biscayne were developed after World War II and cost $9,450. Smathers said yes, and Nixon purchased the first of three homes that became a Nixon compound. During his six years as president, the government spent $10.5 million to make improvements in the name of security, including a $400,000 floating helicopter pad. In 2004, the Nixon home was torn down and replaced with a huge mansion.

Richard Nixon began coming to Florida in 1950 and purchased a home in Key Biscayne after his election as president. He and Pat Nixon welcomed Vice President Spiro Agnew and his wife, Judy.

Throughout the ups and downs of Nixon's life, one thing remained constant: his friendship with Bebe Rebozo. Rebozo died in 1998, four years after Nixon.

GEORGE W. BUSH

The Bush family's connection with Florida dates back almost a century. Prescott Bush, the father of George H.W. Bush and the grandfather of George W. Bush, came to Florida in the 1930s, eventually owning a home in Jupiter. George H.W. Bush came as a child in the 1930s and then returned to train as a World War II pilot in Fort Lauderdale.

George W. Bush came to Florida in 1968 to work in one of the nastiest elections in Florida history. A Republican congressman, Edward Gurney, was challenging one of the state's most respected politicians, Governor Leroy Collins. After serving as governor, Collins agreed to serve as head of the Community Relations Service, which involved working as a go-between for civil rights leaders and local officials. As such, he had a picture taken in Selma, Alabama, with Dr. Martin Luther King Jr. Gurney was convinced that a smear campaign linking Collins with King in a southern state would help defeat him. It worked, as Gurney won easily.

Thirty-two years later, Florida decided the presidency in the contest between Bush and Al Gore. On election night, Gore was the apparent winner in Florida. But in the early morning hours, the situation changed. It now appeared that Bush had carried Florida and the presidency. Then the situation became so confused that no one knew for sure who had won. Questions about irregularities made Florida the center of the nation's attention. For weeks, both sides claimed victory, then the Supreme Court decided the issue, giving the election to Bush.

Florida and Bush are also linked by one of the most dramatic days in the nation's history when he was in Sarasota visiting an elementary school. As

he entered the school, he was told that a plane had crashed into the World Trade Center, but at first it appeared to be an accident. He sat down and began listening to a student read "The Pet Goat." An aide whispered that there had been a second crash and the expression on Bush's face changed dramatically, but he did not want to upset the children, so he remained a few more minutes.

He went to the school's media center and told reporters that there had been "an apparent terrorist attack." He left Sarasota for a roundabout return to Washington.

President George W. Bush was meeting with elementary school children in Sarasota on 9/11 when the two planes crashed into the Twin Towers. His chief of staff, Andrew Card, told him the news.

DONALD TRUMP

For more than 150 years, Florida never had a president. Smaller states sent men to the White House, but Florida never came close. Tiny Vermont had two (Coolidge and Arthur) and Hawaii had one (Obama). Florida never had a major party nominee for president or vice president. Then, in 2019, President Donald Trump changed his legal residence and became a Floridian. For seven decades, he was the quintessential New Yorker, wheeling and dealing in New York real estate. In the 2016 election, he lost New York by a wide margin, and the Democratic governor became a major Trump critic. Florida had certain advantages: it has no income tax or inheritance tax, and the voters were much friendlier to him. Trump carried Florida in 2016 and knew that he needed to carry it in 2020.

Trump had purchased Mar-a-Lago in 1985 in one of the greatest real estate deals in history. Marjorie Merriweather Post, the daughter of the cereal king, built the mansion in the 1920s. When she died, she left the sprawling mansion to the U.S. government. But it was too expensive to maintain, and eventually Trump picked it up for the bargain price of $10 million. He built a giant ballroom and turned the property into a private club.

As president, he became a regular visitor, hosting world leaders and entertaining supporters.

MARY McLEOD BETHUNE HOME

Daytona Beach

Mary McLeod Bethune, a civil rights leader and founder of Bethune-Cookman University, lived in this home from 1913 until her death in 1955. It is located on the campus of the school she built from nothing. An addition, built in 1953, houses the papers of the Bethune Foundation. The house was built around 1904 and acquired by Bethune's school—then called Daytona Educational and Industrial Training School—as Bethune's residence. The house became a major attraction in

Mary Bethune built her college with the help of wealthy and influential friends such as Eleanor Roosevelt.

the 1930s as Bethune's fame grew and she became an adviser to Franklin Roosevelt and friends with the famous, including John D. Rockefeller. The home houses memorabilia from Bethune's life. It is open Monday through Friday, 10:00 a.m. to 3:00 p.m.

Volusia County, Map 5; cookman.edu/foundation; 640 Dr. Mary McLeod Bethune Boulevard, Daytona Beach, Florida, 32114; 386-481-2121.

BOK TOWER GARDENS

Lake Wales

The Bok Tower, with its pealing bells, is located in some of Florida lushest gardens. Lake Wales is off the beaten path, but Bok Tower is worth a detour.

Edward W. Bok came to the United States from the Netherlands when he was six. He became the publisher of the *Ladies' Home Journal* and an advocate for world peace. He was grateful for the opportunities he found in the United States and wanted to make a gift to the nation. He became wealthy and built a home in Lake Wales near Iron Mountain. It is a mountain by Florida standards, rising 295 feet above sea level. He purchased the property and built a tower with a sixty-bell carillon and surrounding gardens. He called it "a spot of beauty second to none in the country." He gave it as a gift to the American people, and President Calvin Coolidge accepted it at dedication ceremonies in 1929. The grounds were laid out by Frederick Law Olmsted Jr., the nation's most famous landscape architect. The tower is open 365 days a year from 8:00 a.m. to 6:00 p.m. The concerts are daily at 1:00 and 3:00 p.m., but short songs are played on the hour and half hour.

Polk County, Map 1; boktowergardens.org; 1151 Tower Boulevard, Lake Wales, Florida, 33853; 863-676-1408.

BRITISH FORT

Sumatra

Built during the War of 1812 and also known as Negro Fort, this was the location of a fort occupied by runaway slaves as well as Indians. Due to a massive explosion near the end of the war, nothing remains of the fort. The land in the Florida Panhandle was the site of two forts. The first, known as Negro Fort, was built in 1814 by the British and destroyed by a magazine explosion. In 1818, Fort Gadsden was built within the walls of the old fort. Because the fort is known by many names—among them Prospect Bluff, Fort Blount, African Fort and Fort Apalachicola—it is easy to get confused. It was called Negro Fort because it became a refuge for slaves escaping from Georgia and the Carolinas. Despite its rich history, there is little to see at the site. It is off State Road 65 in the Apalachicola National Forest near Sumatra.

Franklin County, Map 3; fs.usda.gov/recrea/applachicola; Sumatra, Florida, 32321; 850-643-2282.

CAPE CANAVERAL AIR FORCE STATION

Cocoa

In 1947, Cape Canaveral Air Force Station was chosen as the United States Missile Testing Range. Earlier sites near the West Coast had proven unacceptable. The first missile—actually a German V-2 rocket—went up in 1950. A series of rocket programs led to the first manned flight in 1961, when Alan Shepard soared into space on *Freedom 7*. The station was used for all the Mercury flights and several of the Gemini flights. As the space program progressed, the station was phased out and replaced by the nearby John F. Kennedy Space Center. The museum has limited access for visitors.

In 1950, the first missile was launched from Florida's east coast, sending the United States into the Space Age.

It is open for tours Wednesday through Sunday and, because of security concerns, is highly regulated. Visitors must register at the visitor complex between 9:00 and 11:00 a.m., and identification is required.

Brevard County, Map 5; afspacemuseum.org/visit; 191 Museum Circle, Cape Canaveral, Florida, 32920; 321-853-9171.

CATHEDRAL OF ST. AUGUSTINE

St. Augustine

St. Augustine is where the Christian faith began in what is now the continental United States. The first Spanish to arrive in 1565 began to establish a Catholic church. The first church was small and crude and burned down during an English invasion. A second church was built, but it was destroyed by fire as well. As the 1600s began, funds were raised in Spain to construct a true cathedral utilizing professional architects and workmen. The third church survived for nearly a century before it burned down. In 1783, work on a massive cathedral was begun. The enormous structure suffered huge damage in 1887, and a new cathedral rose from the ruins. The cathedral is open year-round.

St. Johns County, Map 2; thefirstparish.org; 38 Cathedral Place, St. Augustine, Florida, 32084; 904-824-2806.

CRYSTAL RIVER SITE

Crystal River

This is one of the longest-occupied sites in North America. Nearly ten thousand years ago, Crystal River was home to Paleo-Indians, a nomadic people who came to the area for food. About eight thousand years ago, the ice caps in North America began to melt, and rising seas and the ice age creatures began to disappear. The descendants of the Paleo-Indians put down roots and created communities. There is a ceremonial center and burial complex occupied during the Deptford, Weeden Island and Safety Harbor periods. Today, it is best known as home to the manatees and is a state park covering more than 27,500 acres. There are directed boat rides and trails to hike.

Visitors can swim with the manatees—the ticket prices start at two dollars. The park is open 365 days a year from 8:00 a.m. to sunset.

Citrus County, Map 7; floridastateparks.org; 3400 North Museum Point, Crystal River, Florida, 34428; 352-228-6028.

DADE BATTLEFIELD

Bushnell

On December 28, 1835, Major Francis Dade and 110 soldiers from Fort Brooke (Tampa) were marching to Fort King (Ocala) when they were attacked by 180 Seminole Indians and nearly wiped out. Just 3 soldiers survived, although one of them was pursued by a Seminole Indian and killed. Many of the dead were buried in St. Augustine. The battle launched the longest Indian war in American history. In January, there is a reenactment of the battle. The state park is open from 8:00 a.m. to 5:00 p.m. 365 days a year.

Sumter County, Map 5; floridastateparks.org; 7200 County Road 603, Bushnell, Florida, 33513; 352-793-4781.

MARJORY STONEMAN DOUGLAS HOUSE

Coconut Grove

Marjory Stoneman Douglas was born six years before Miami was created and lived long enough to see the city celebrate its centennial. She worked for the *Miami Herald*, where her father was an editor, and quickly branched out to write for magazines.

Marjory Stoneman Douglas was an early crusader for the environment in Florida. She wrote about the importance of the Everglades long before anyone else was paying attention to its vital role in Florida.

In 1947, she published her greatest work, *The Everglades: River of Grass.* Most dismissed the Everglades as a swamp that was best paved over and developed. She launched a crusade to preserve it, and it became one of the early environmental icons. Her home at 3744 Stewart Avenue in Coconut Grove was built in 1926 and resembles an English cottage. Not only did Douglas do her writing in the nine-hundred-square-foot house, but it was also a center for environmental activity. The state purchased the home at 3744 Stewart Avenue in 1991, although she continued to live there until her death in 1998. Currently the home is not open to the public.

Miami-Dade County, Map 6.

EL CENTRO ESPAÑOL DE TAMPA

Tampa

Home of the first mutual aid society in Florida and part of the Ybor City Historic District, this site is located in Tampa's Ybor City neighborhood. Immigrants from Spain and Cuba flocked to the building beginning in 1891, and the club welcomed tens of thousands of people to the city and

In the late 1800s, revolutions in Cuba forced thousands of Cubans to flee to Florida. In 1885, Cuban cigar makers founded Ybor City, a center for dozens of cigar factories that employed the new arrivals and created a booming community. Much of it remains as it was more than a century ago.

a new life. The present building, built in 1912, replaced a smaller building. Over the years, the membership in the club, which peaked at 2,600, began to decline as immigration slowed and residents moved beyond Ybor City. Today, the building at 1526 East Seventh Avenue houses a restaurant and is open to the public.

Hillsborough County, Map 7; centroespanoltampa.org; 1526 East Seventh Avenue, Tampa, Florida, 33605; 813-870-0559.

"FERDINAND MAGELLAN"

Miami

The "Ferdinand Magellan" served as the presidential rail car from 1943 until 1958. It was built in 1929 as a private rail car as part of a group named for famous explorers. At the start of World War II, President Franklin Roosevelt's press secretary, Steve Early, recommended that the president secure a special car with state-of-the-art security equipment. The car was wrapped in armor, and bullet-resistant glass was installed. There was even a primitive system of air conditioning. The car was added to the presidential train. The connection to Florida came on the car's first presidential trip. Roosevelt traveled from Washington to Miami, where he boarded a plane for the trip to a conference in Casablanca. After Roosevelt's death, his special wheelchair lift was removed. President Harry Truman made the car even more famous during the 1948 campaign when he used the train for his whistle-stop campaign. One of history's most famous photographs was taken of Truman holding a copy of the *Chicago Tribune* with the erroneous headline "Dewey Defeats Truman." The car was used by President Dwight Eisenhower a few times, but the air age arrived and the car was finally removed from service in 1954. It came out of retirement just once, used by President Ronald Reagan during his 1984 reelection campaign. In 1958, the car was acquired by the Gold Coast Railroad Museum.

Miami-Dade County, Map 6; goldcoastrailroadmuseum.org; 12450 Southwest 152nd Street, Miami, 33177; 305-253-0063.

FLORIDA SOUTHERN COLLEGE HISTORIC DISTRICT

Lakeland

Florida Southern College traces its roots to 1883, when it was founded in Orlando as the South Florida Institute, which makes it the oldest four-year college in Florida. Several moves later, it settled in Lakeland in 1922. It would have remained a small, respected college if not for architect Frank Lloyd Wright. In 1938, the college hired Wright to design a new campus. He started with the chapel, which opened in 1941, and it soon became the largest collection of Wright buildings in a single place. It is a mecca for those who love Wright's architecture. When new buildings were needed, the school hired the famed architect Robert A.M. Stern, who pledged to "honor Wright's historic legacy." The college offers tours of the campus and has a building dedicated to Wright's architecture with a gift shop.

Polk County, Map 1; flsouthern.edu/community/frank-lloyd-wright/home.aspx; 111 Lake Hollingsworth Drive, Lakeland, Florida, 33801; 863-680-4597.

Florida Southern College was the first college in Florida but moved several times before settling in Lakeland, where Frank Lloyd Wright designed a magnificent campus.

FORT KING SITE

Ocala

Fort King, located near Ocala, was built in 1827 as tensions with the Seminole Indians increased. When war came, it became a key outpost for troops. Major Francis Dade was going to Fort King when his regiment was attacked and slaughtered by the Seminoles. In 1836, the fort was burned by the Seminoles and rebuilt the following year. The commanding generals at the fort included future president Zachary Taylor. When the Second Seminole War ended, the fort was abandoned, and the lumber from the fort was salvaged by nearby residents and used in other buildings. The fort has been rebuilt to resemble the original fort.

Marion County, Map 5; ocalafl.org/government/city-departments-j-z/recreation-parks/ fort-king-national-historic-landmark; 3925 East Fort King Street, Ocala, Florida, 34470; 352-368-5535.

FORT MOSE SITE

St. Augustine

In 1693, Spanish King Charles II decreed that runaway slaves from British colonies be given sanctuary in Spanish colonies. As word spread through Georgia and the Carolinas, hundreds of slaves made their way to St. Augustine. In 1738, the Spanish governor of Florida issued a charter for the first free African American settlement in North America. It was named Gracia Real de Santa Teresa de Mosa, or Fort Mose. When the British took over Florida in 1763, the fort and surrounding village were abandoned. Visitors can see the area, learn about one of the most intriguing settlements of the 1700s and, once a month, see a militia muster. There is a visitor center and museum.

St. Johns County, Map 2; floridastateparks.org; 15 Fort Mose Trail, St. Augustine, Florida, 32084; 904-823-2232.

FORT SAN CARLOS DE BARRANCAS
Pensacola

The site of this fort has been occupied by four nations and seen many battles. The Spanish were the first, building Fort San Carlos de Austria on the site in 1698. Indians attacked unsuccessfully in 1707, and in 1719, the French captured the original fort and burned it. The British took over the fort and held it until the Spanish retook West Florida in 1781. They built a new fort, San Carlos de Barrancas. The fort saw combat again when the British fought the Americans during the War of 1812. In 1818, the Americans attacked the Spanish and took the fort. The U.S. government expanded the fort, and it saw action again during the Civil War, when the Confederates and Union forces fought. New weapons developed during the Civil War made the masonry fort outdated. The fort becoming obsolete coincided with the rise of the airplane, and the navy turned the area into a Naval Air Station and used it to train pilots for World War I. The fort was deactivated in 1947. The fort site is now part of the Gulf Islands National Seashore. Fort Barrancas has been restored and is open to the public.

Escambia County, Map 3; nps.gov/guis/learn/historyculture/fort-barrancas.htm; 3182 Taylor Road, Pensacola, Florida, 32508; 850-455-5167.

Historic Fort San Carlos and Fort Barrancas, Pensacola, Fla.

Fort San Carlos has been occupied by a number of armies and battles, beginning with the Spanish fighting Native Americans.

FORT SAN MARCOS DE APALACHE

St. Marks

It is hard to imagine today, but at one time St. Marks was one of the largest cities in Florida, a shipping and military center. In 1679, the Spanish built a wooden fort, and the protection of the fort soon drew settlers. A newer fort was built in the mid-1750s, but a hurricane destroyed it and drowned the soldiers inside. The Spanish built a stone fort in 1759, but when the British took over Florida, the Spanish abandoned the fort. In 1783, Spain reclaimed Florida and the fort. During raids against the Seminole Indians in 1818, Andrew Jackson captured the fort and held it for a year. When the United States acquired Florida in 1821, it retook the fort. The U.S. government expanded the fort and established a hospital for seamen. The Confederates seized the fort and held it until the end of the Civil War. The fort fell into disrepair, and today there are only remains of the fort. There is a museum and visitor center, and tours of the area are given.

Wakulla County, Map 3; floridastateparks.org; 148 Old Fort Road, St. Marks, Florida, 32355; 850-925-6216.

FORT WALTON MOUND

Fort Walton Beach

There are three large surviving mounds in the Panhandle left from the era when tribes were the only residents of Florida. The Fort Walton Mound is 12 feet high and 223 feet wide at the base. The mounds were built in the center of the Indian village and were the center of life in the village. The mound was a platform for the temple and the chief's residence, as well as the burial site for village leaders. Over the years, the mound became higher. There is discrepancy over when the mound began. Some date it to AD 800, others to about AD 1500. It was abandoned around 1600, but the reason remains a mystery. The area remained uninhabited until the mid-1800s, when settlers began moving into the area. Today, there are several museums, including the Indian Temple Mound Museum, the Camp Walton Schoolhouse Museum, the Garnier Post Office Museum and a Civil War Exhibits Building. The schoolhouse dates to 1911 and is a rare example of a one-room schoolhouse. The Indian Temple Mound Museum contains examples of pre-Columbian artifacts from the mound and exhibits of Native American and Florida history. The post office museum is an example of a rural post office and dates to the early 1900s. The mound was a base for Confederate soldiers during the Civil War, and the Civil War exhibits building has displays about Florida during the war.

Walton County, Map 3; fwb.org/parksrec/page/Indian-temple-mound-museum; 139 Miracle Strep Parkway Southeast, Fort Walton Beach, Florida, 32548; 850-833-9595.

FORT ZACHARY TAYLOR

Key West

Fort Zachary Taylor was one of the forts built in the mid-1800s to protect the southeast coast of the United States. The United States acquired Florida in 1821 and knew that it would need forts. Planning for the first fort, in Key West, began in 1822, but the process of approval and building was slow. Construction finally began in 1845, but the work was slow and delayed by yellow fever, shortages of bricks and weather. It was finished in 1845 and named for President Zachary Taylor five months after his death in 1850. The fort was first used in the Civil War when Union troops occupied it, and it was later used to discourage Confederate blockade runners. The Spanish-American War led to significant changes in the fort. It was also occupied by troops during World War I, World War II and the Cuban Missile Crisis. The army turned the fort over to the navy in 1947, and in the 1960s, volunteers began excavating the grounds and found cannons and ammunition. The fort is a little-known attraction but is one of the best in Florida.

Monroe County, Map 6; fortzacharytaylor.com; 601 Howard England Way, Key West, Florida, 33040; 305-292-6713.

FREEDOM TOWER

Miami

This building has been part of Miami's history for a century and remains an iconic part of the city. After losing the presidency in 1920, James Cox purchased the *Miami Metropolis*, the largest newspaper in the booming city. He changed the name to the *Miami Daily News*, and in 1925, he published the largest newspaper ever, 508 pages. The same year, he built a sprawling building to house his newspaper. The building housed the newspaper for nearly thirty years until it moved to a new plant in 1957. The building was empty for several years until Fidel Castro took power in Cuba. Thousands of Cubans fled the island, and officials in Miami were overwhelmed. The federal government took over the building to process the new arrivals and provide them services. Once the immigration rate had slowed by 1972, the building was sold to private investors. Today, it is owned by Miami-Dade College and used as a museum and cultural center.

Miami-Dade County, Map 6; mdcmoad.org/freedom-tower; 600 Biscayne Boulevard, Miami, Florida, 33132; 305-237-7700.

GONZALEZ-ALVAREZ HOUSE
St. Augustine

Lots of things in Florida claim to be the oldest, but the Gonzalez-Alvarez House in St. Augustine really is the oldest surviving house in St. Augustine. It dates to about 1763 and started as a one-story structure when occupied by a Spanish militiaman. When the British took over Florida, a British major added a second wood-frame story and glass windows. The St. Augustine Historical Society purchased the house in 1918 and began restoring it to its late nineteenth-century appearance.

St. Johns County, Map 2; saintaugustinehistoricalsociety.org; 14 Francis Street, St. Augustine, Florida, 32084; 904-824-2872.

The Gonzalez-Alvarez House in St. Augustine is more than 250 years old and is now home to the St. Augustine Historical Society.

GOVERNOR STONE SCHOONER

Panama City

This schooner was launched in 1877 in Mississippi and named for a Mississippi governor. It passed through a series of owners, surviving storms and even a sinking. During World War II, the ship was used for training by the Merchant Marine Academy. Restored in the 1960s, it is one of just five surviving two-masted coasting cargo schooners. Hurricane Michael in 2018 did extensive damage to the ship, and restoration efforts are ongoing.

Bay County, Map 3; governorstone.org; St. Andrews Marina, 3151 West 10th Street, Panama City, Florida, 32401; 850-872-7240.

ERNEST HEMINGWAY HOUSE

Key West

Ernest Hemingway only lived in his Key West house for eight years but continued to own it until his death in 1961. The house has the richest history on the island. It stands just sixteen feet above sea level, but it is the second-highest point on the island. It was built in 1851 by Asa Tift, a wrecker who made his fortune salvaging wrecks off the coast. The house was the first on the island to have indoor plumbing. Hemingway and his wife, Pauline, lived in the house and made significant, even humorous, changes. The couple purchased the house at a tax auction for $8,000—money that came from

Ernest Hemingway came to Key West to pick up a car and ended up buying a house and falling in love with the island.

Pauline's wealthy uncle. While Hemingway was away reporting on the Spanish Civil War, his wife installed an outrageously expensive swimming pool. He was unpleasantly surprised when he returned and exclaimed, "Well, you might as well have my last cent." He threw a penny into the wet cement, and it remains there today. He built a wall around the yard for privacy as the home became the island's leading tourist attraction. He set up a boxing ring in the backyard and found local fighters for bouts. His strangest addition was to insert a discarded urinal from his favorite bar, Sloppy Joe's, into a fountain in the yard. It is there today. The house had a new burst of fame in 1988 when part of the James Bond movie *License to Kill* was filmed there. It was also shown in the 2017 movie *The Leisure Seeker*.

Monroe County, Map 6; hemingwayhome.com; 907 Whitehead Street, Key West, Florida, 33040; 305-294-1136.

HOTEL PONCE DE LEON

St. Augustine

This was the first true luxury hotel in Florida and the beginning of Florida as an attraction for the very wealthy. It was also the first hotel in the nation to have electricity installed during construction, with Thomas Edison supplying the DC generators. The hotel was the dream of oil millionaire Henry Flagler, the partner of John D. Rockefeller in the creation of Standard Oil Company. Flagler hired only the best to build and furnish his masterpiece. The New York architects John Carrere and Thomas Hastings designed the hotel. Louis Comfort Tiffany and his associates at Tiffany & Company supervised the interior design and provided the beautiful stained-glass windows in the dining room. The Ponce opened in 1888 and drew large crowds. Flagler was convinced that Florida could become the "American Riviera." During World War II, the Ponce de Leon was used as a Coast Guard Training Center—one of the towers was a brig—and housed as many as 2,500 recruits at a time. As Flagler developed hotels farther south, the attraction of the Ponce de Leon declined. Flagler's two other hotels in St. Augustine closed, but the Ponce de Leon kept going. When the war ended, the hotel reopened, initially to large crowds. But the boom did not last, and by the 1960s, it was in financial trouble. The hotel dealt with the effects of the civil rights

Henry Flagler built the magnificent Ponce de Leon Hotel for his wealthy friends. It revived the sleepy fishing village of St. Augustine.

movement, including occupations by demonstrations demanding that the hotel integrate. It closed in 1967 and in 1968 was given to the newly established Flagler College.

St. Johns County, Map 2; legacy.flagler.edu; 74 King Street, St. Augustine, Florida, 32084; 904-823-3378.

ZORA NEALE HURSTON HOUSE

Fort Pierce

The story of how Zora Neale Hurston came to live in this small home in Fort Pierce is one of the saddest ever. The house has nothing to distinguish it— concrete block construction with a stucco exterior and a gravel roof. Hurston grew up in Eatonville, about 120 miles away. She became one of the leading

African American writers of the 1920s, part of the Harlem Renaissance. Her best-known work is *Their Eyes Were Watching God*. Her writing influenced Toni Morrison, Alice Walker and Maya Angelou, among others. Her books created a sensation but gradually fell out of favor, and her fame declined. She drifted through jobs, and her finances became precarious. By the 1950s, she was working as a maid in South Florida. C.E. Bolen, the publisher of the African American newspaper the *Fort Pierce Chronicle*, urged her to move to Fort Pierce, and at the age of sixty-five, she embarked on a new career as a columnist. She wrote about everything from cowboys to voodoo. Dr. C.C. Benton, an old family friend from Eatonville, let her stay rent-free in the two-bedroom home for two years. For the last year of her life, she stayed at the St. Lucie County Welfare Home, a final stop for the poor, elderly and sick. She died there, alone and forgotten, in 1960. Her death passed nearly unnoticed, and she was buried in an unmarked grave at Fort Pierce. In 1973, a young Alice Walker—her classic *The Color Purple* was still nine years in the future—came to Fort Pierce to find out about Hurston. Walker found out about the unmarked grave and purchased a tombstone for Hurston. It read:

> *Zora Neale Hurston*
> *A Genius of the South*
> *1901–1960*
> *Novelist, Folklorist*
> *Anthropologist*

Gradually, Hurston's work once again became popular, and she became required reading in school throughout the country. In 2005, Oprah Winfrey selected *Their Eyes Were Watching God* as her book choice. The welfare home is at 809 North 9th Street. Today, it is a community center. Her last home is at 1734 Avenue L.

St. Lucie County, Map 4; cityoffortpierce.com; 772-467-3000.

USCGC INGHAM

Key West

The *Ingham*, named for Secretary of the Treasury Samuel D. Ingham, was the most decorated vessel in the Coast Guard and the recipient of two

Presidential Unit Citations. Built at the Philadelphia Naval Shipyard and launched in 1936, it served from World War II through Vietnam. Originally, it was acquired for display in Charleston, South Carolina. In 2009, it was moved to Key West to be part of the Key West Maritime Memorial Museum. The ship has special significance for Coast Guard veterans: it is a national memorial for the 912 members of the Coast Guard who died in World War II and Vietnam. Their names are on a memorial plaque on the ship's quarterdeck.

Monroe County, Map 6; uscgcingham.org; West End of Southard Street, Key West, Florida, 33041; 305-395-9554.

LLAMBIAS HOUSE

St. Augustine

The Llambias house is one of the handful of surviving homes built during the first period of Spanish Florida. It was built before 1783, but no one is sure exactly when. After the French and Indian War, the British took over Florida from the Spanish in 1763. At the time, the house had just one story, made from plastered coquina limestone. The kitchen was in a separate building. In 1777, a second floor was added, along with windows. The home was given to the city in 1954 and was renovated. Today, it is run by the St. Augustine Historical Society. The beautiful gardens have become a major site for weddings, and the home is a key stop for tourists visiting the town.

St. Johns County, Map 2; saintaugustinehistoricalsociety.org; 31 St. Francis Street, St. Augustine, Florida, 32084; 904-824-2872.

MAPLE LEAF

Mandarin

The *Maple Leaf* began as a typical side-wheel steamship when it was launched in 1851 in Upper Canada. For a decade, it carried cargo and passengers. During the Civil War, the United States chartered the ship to transport soldiers and military equipment. As the ship crossed the St. Johns River near Jacksonville on April 1, 1864, it struck a Confederate torpedo (today called a mine), inflicting major damage and killing four crew members. It was the first use of a mine to damage a ship and introduced a new and deadly weapon to naval warfare. The ship could not be salvaged, and most of it sank beneath the water. Its position in the St. Johns River made it a threat to navigation, and the U.S. Army Corps of Engineers removed the top of the ship in the 1880s. In 1984, an archaeological expedition found what was left of the ship below the water. It is remarkably well preserved and a favorite of divers.

Duval County, Map 2; mandarinmuseum.net; 11964 Mandarin Road, Jacksonville, Florida, 32223; 904-268-0784.

MAR-A-LAGO

Palm Beach

This massive estate has had two of the best-known owners in the world: Marjorie Merriweather Post and Donald Trump. Post was born in 1887, the daughter of C.W. Post, the founder of what has become the Post Cereal Company. She was just twenty-seven years old when her father died, leaving her the company and making her the richest woman in the world. The company kept growing, along with her fortune and her desire to spend money on residences. In 1924, she and her then husband, Edward Hutton, founder of the financial firm E.F. Hutton, began construction on a 126-room mansion covering sixty-two thousand square feet. Construction took three years, and when it was finished, it was the largest private home in the United States. When Post died in 1973, she willed the property to the National Park Service to use as a residence for visiting heads of state or as a winter White House. She also left funds to maintain the house, but they did not cover the cost. In 1981, the government returned the home to her foundation. The Post family once again found itself with a home it did not want, along with very expensive maintenance costs. At a price of $20 million, it went unsold. The city approved plans to tear down the mansion and build smaller homes. Donald Trump purchased some nearby property and said that he would build a home blocking the Mar-a-Lago view of the ocean. The price dropped to $10 million, and the family accepted his bid.

Marjorie Merriweather Post inherited her father's vast cereal empire and used some of the money to build the magnificent Mar-a-Lago in Palm Beach. It was later sold to Donald Trump, who turned it into an exclusive club.

He added a twenty-thousand-square-foot ballroom and kept part of it for a private residence, turning the remainder into a private club. It is closed to the public.

Palm Beach County; Map 4; 1100 South Ocean Boulevard, Palm Beach, Florida; 33480.

PENSACOLA NAVAL AIR STATION HISTORIC DISTRICT

Pensacola

When the Pensacola Naval Air Station opened in 1913, most people doubted that air power would ever be a factor in war—today, no one does. The sprawling air base, known as the "Cradle of Naval Aviation," is the undisputed leader in air training. The site began with a wooden fort in 1697 and survived an Indian attack before being destroyed by the French in 1719. British colonists took over the site in 1763, and in 1781, the Spanish took it back and built a new fort in 1797. General Andrew Jackson captured the fort in 1814 during the War of 1812, and later the British destroyed the fort. Spain came back and held the area until the United States acquired Florida in 1821. Four years later, the Pensacola Navy Yard was approved. When the base opened in 1914, there were 6 pilots, 23 enlisted men and seven seaplanes. When the United States entered World War II in 1917, the air station consisted of 38 aviators, 163 enlisted men and fifty-four aircraft. The base ballooned to 438 officers and 5,538 enlisted men by the time the war ended eighteen months later. It became known as the "Annapolis of the Air," as it became the central point for training pilots. Today, the original eighty-two-acre site includes parts of the old navy yard, structures from the early days of training and buildings dating back a century and a half. In all, there are fifty-five buildings on the site.

Escambia County, Map 3; nps.gov/articles/Pensacola-naval-air-station-historic-district. htm; 1540 South Blue Angel Parkway, Pensacola, Florida, 32507; 800-327-5002.

PLAZA FERDINAND VII

Pensacola

The plaza is an outdoor garden and park in the Historic Pensacola Village section of downtown Pensacola. It is the site where Spain formally transferred Florida to the United States in 1821. It covers just two acres and was originally named for Ferdinand VII, the king of Spain from 1813 to 1833. The area was first laid out by the British in 1765, when they controlled West Florida and Pensacola was its capital. When the Spanish retook control after the American Revolution, they named the park but also reduced it in size, selling off portions in 1802. On July 21, 1821, Andrew Jackson watched as the Spanish flag was lowered and the American flag raised. Jackson was inaugurated as the first territorial governor. Today, it has a fountain and tributes to Jackson and William Dudley Chipley, the man who opened West Florida with his railroads.

Escambia County, Map 3; cityofpensacola.com; 300 South Palafox Street, Pensacola, Florida, 32502; 850-206-7231.

PONCE DE LEON INLET LIGHT STATION

Ponce Inlet

This is the tallest lighthouse in Florida at 175 feet and one of the tallest remaining lighthouses in the nation. (Cape Hatteras holds the record at 207 feet.) The lighthouse site dates to 1835, when a lighthouse was built but never used. The oil to provide the light never came, and a vicious storm washed away part of the foundation. An 1835 Indian attack smashed the lantern glass and burned the wooden stairs. The lighthouse soon collapsed. It was the 1880s before another attempt was made to build a lighthouse ten miles south of Daytona Beach. The construction of the second lighthouse has its own fantastic history. Orville Babcock was a close friend and military aide to Ulysses S. Grant during the Civil War. When Grant became president, he named Babcock his top aide. Babcock turned out to be a crook and was indicted twice. To allow him to escape the scandals of Washington, Grant named him lighthouse inspector, which took him to Florida. He supervised the construction of the new lighthouse until he drowned not far from the lighthouse in 1884. Three years later, the lighthouse was finally finished, and the light turned on.

Ponce Inlet Lighthouse has a rich history and is the nation's second-tallest lighthouse.

In 1897, Stephen Crane, the author of the classic *The Red Badge of Courage*, was sailing from Jacksonville to cover the growing revolution in Cuba. His ship sank in a storm and he escaped in a dinghy. Guided by the light from the Mosquito Inlet Lighthouse, he steered for shore. He wrote about the ordeal in *The Open Boat*. In 1970, the Coast Guard abandoned the lighthouse and built a new one at New Smyrna Beach. A local group took over the lighthouse in 1972, and restoration began on the lighthouse and the buildings around it. It is 203 steps to the top, and for $1.25 you can purchase a certificate to prove to the world that you made it to the top.

Volusia County, Map 5; ponceinlet.org; 4931 South Peninsula Drive, Ponce Inlet, Florida, 32127; 386-761-1821.

MARJORIE KINNAN RAWLINGS HOUSE AND FARM YARD

Cross Creek

From this simple farmhouse, Marjorie Kinnan Rawlings wrote her classic novel *The Yearling*. In 1928, she and her husband, also a writer, moved to Cross Creek in the middle of Florida to find solitude for their work. They purchased a seventy-four-acre citrus farm, and Marjorie fell in love with the farm and people of the area. Her husband was not as enamored, and the marriage dissolved. She began writing for magazines, centering her stories on life in Cross Creek. In 1933, her first novel about life in Florida, *South Moon Under*, brought her fame. Five years later, her seminal work, *The Yearling*, came out, earning her a Pulitzer Prize and a movie contract. She became friends with Ernest Hemingway and Robert Frost. After her marriage ended, she married her friend Norton Baskin, who owned a hotel

Marjorie Kinnan Rawlings sought solitude to write when she moved to Cross Creek. She found colorful people to populate her books and won the Pulitzer Prize.

in St. Augustine. After 1941, she spent most of her time in St. Augustine and at a cottage in Crescent Beach. The Cross Creek home has a main residence, a kitchen/dining room and the guest cottage. Rawlings added bathrooms and created a large screened porch where she would sit and write. It is furnished just as it was when she lived there.

Alachua County, Map 2; floridastateparks.org; 18700 South County Road 325, Cross Creek, Florida, 32640; 352-466-3672.

THE RESEARCH STUDIO

Maitland

Today, it is known as the Art & History Museums, but when artist Andre Smith founded the center as an artist colony in 1937, he called it the Research Studio. Smith wanted it to become a center for experimental art, with financial support from Mary Curtis Bok, the daughter of Cyrus Curtis, the founder of the *Ladies' Home Journal*, and the wife of Edward Bok, who donated the money for the Bok Tower in Lake Wales. With more than two hundred carvings and reliefs, it is an important example of Art Deco fantasy and Mayan Revival architecture in the United States. Today, the Maitland Art Center encompasses five museums. The architecture is known as Mayan Revival or Fantasy Architecture.

Orange County, Map 5; artandhistory.org; 231 West Parkwood Avenue, Maitland, Florida, 32751; 407-539-2181.

SAFETY HARBOR SITE

Safety Harbor

Known as the Safety Harbor Site, it contains the largest surviving mound in the Tampa Bay area. It is part of Philippe Park and contains a large temple mound, two shell middens and one smaller burial mount. The temple mound is 150 feet in diameter and nearly 20 feet high. As with other Indian mounds, it contains a number of levels built of sand and shells. When the Spanish arrived, it was the capital of the Tocobaga tribe. European diseases wiped out many of the Indians, and by 1700, the tribe had abandoned the site. Although its existence was known, it was not until 1929 that excavation began. The findings have included pottery similar to the pottery found around Fort Walton.

Pinellas County, Map 7; safetyharbor.com/Philippe-Park/Indian-Mound; 940 7th Street South, Safety Harbor, Florida, 34695; 727-669-1947.

SAN LUIS DE TALIMALI

Tallahassee

One of the major reasons the Spanish settled Florida was to convert the native tribes to Catholicism. They began around St. Augustine and soon expanded to the Florida Panhandle. The San Luis de Talimali, also known as the Mission San Luis de Apalachee, is located about two miles from the Florida Capitol Building in Tallahassee. The friars preached to the Timucua and Apalachee Indians. A sprawling complex was built including a council house that could hold more than two thousand people. It was the largest council house in the Southeast. The mission survived for nearly seventy years until it was evacuated to avoid an attack by Indians and settlers from South Carolina. The friars destroyed the fort rather than have it fall into their hands.

Leon County, Map 3; trailoffloridasindianheritage.org/mission-san-luis; 2100 West Tennessee Street, Tallahassee, Florida, 32304; 850-245-64006.

ST. AUGUSTINE TOWN PLAN
HISTORIC DISTRICT

St. Augustine

The St. Augustine Town Plan Historic District is packed with history dating back more than four hundred years. The district includes the original site of St. Augustine, which was built between the mid-sixteenth century and the early nineteenth century. The district's boundaries are roughly those of the original town of St. Augustine and cover the period of development between

1672 and 1935. The Historic District is bounded by Orange Street, San Marcos Street, the Matanzas River, St. Francis Street and Cordova Street.

St. Johns County, Map 2; citystaug.com; 904-825-1000.

TAMPA BAY HOTEL

Tampa

The two railroad barons of Florida were Henry Flagler and Henry Plant. The men maintained a friendly rivalry but chose different paths. Flagler concentrated on Florida's east coast, creating a railroad stretching from Jacksonville to Key West. Plant went to the west coast, with his empire based in Tampa. He built the 511-room Tampa Bay Hotel in 1891. Like Flagler, Plant built many hotels, and this was one of eight. Plant installed Florida's first elevator—it is still working today. Plant went to Europe to find items to decorate his hotel and complement the unusual architecture of his hotel. In 1898, Tampa became the headquarters for the army's campaign for the Spanish-American War. Thousands of soldiers poured into Tampa, and the

Henry Plant's Tampa Bay Hotel was the headquarters for the military during the Spanish-American War and later became the University of Tampa.

156

Henry Plant invented the all-inclusive vacation—one price bought train fare, hotels and meals.

hotel was used by the commanding officers, military officials and reporters. Strategy for the war was planned in the hotel. Colonel Theodore Roosevelt was one of those who stayed in the hotel while he commanded his Rough Riders. The hotel closed in 1930 as the Great Depression reduced tourism. For three years, it was empty, and in 1933, Tampa Junior College moved in and became the University of Tampa. In 1941, the City of Tampa signed a ninety-nine-year lease with the university to use part of the building for a museum and to guarantee that it was preserved in its original state.

Hillsborough County, Map 7; plantmuseum.com; 401 West Kennedy Boulevard, Tampa, Florida, 33606; 813-254-1891.

VIZCAYA

Miami

James Deering McCormick was the owner of the huge Deering McCormick-International Harvester and one of the richest men in the country. Deering was also an early environmentalist, and when he purchased 180 acres in Miami around 1912, he preserved the trees and mangrove swamps on the property. He built a large villa and magnificent gardens and opened his mansion on Christmas Day 1916, although construction continued until 1922. Deering used it as his winter residence until his death in 1925. He left the property to his two nieces, who struggled to maintain it. Hurricanes damaged the property, and the nieces began to sell off portions of the land, including 50 acres to build Mercy Hospital. In 1952, Dade County acquired the estate and gardens for $1 million. The following year, it opened as the Dade County Art Museum.

Dade County, Map 6; vizcaya.org; 3251 South Miami Avenue, Miami, Florida, 33129; 305-250-9133.

WHITEHALL

Palm Beach

It was the ultimate wedding gift! Henry Flagler gave his new bride the most magnificent house in Florida. Flagler's first wife had died in 1881 at the age of forty, and two years later, he remarried. When his second wife went insane, he divorced her and married Mary Lily Kenan Flagler. They lived together in the house from 1902 until Flagler's death in 1913. For two decades, Flagler had been working his way south, beginning in Jacksonville. He came to Palm Beach and decided that it would be the perfect spot for his ultimate development: a beautiful island for his wealthy friends. On the mainland, he built West Palm Beach for his railroad workers and for those who would care for the wealthy of Palm Beach. As Flagler developed his Florida empire, his buildings were located away from the ocean, including Whitehall. The popularity of the beach was still in the future. In 1912, Flagler fell down a flight of stairs at Whitehall and never recovered. He died the following year. Following his death, the home was closed for three years. Mary Flagler returned to the house just once, with her new husband, Robert Worth Bingham. Mary died later that year and left Whitehall to her niece, Louise Lewis, who sold it to a group of investors that added an eleven-story tower and turned the entire residence into a hotel. In 1959, there was talk of tearing down Whitehall, but Flagler's granddaughter Jean Matthews formed an organization to purchase the property; in 1960, it reopened as a museum.

Palm Beach County, Map 4; flaglermuseum.us; 1 Whitehall Way, Palm Beach, Florida, 33480; 561-655-2833.

WINDOVER ARCHAEOLOGICAL SITE

Titusville

Nearly seven thousand years ago, the land near Titusville was occupied by natives. In 1982, a new housing development, Windover Farms, was being built when a backhoe operator uncovered several skulls. The medical examiner found that the remains were not recent. The developers called in archaeologists, and radiocarbon placed the bones as being more than seven thousand years old. The developers set the land aside for future exploration.

The bones were in a peat deposit, which preserved the remains. It turned out to be one of the largest New World collections of human skeletal material from the period, along with fiber arts. Researchers faced a daunting task: the remains were buried about six feet down under a layer of dirt and water. The bodies ranged from infants to some sixty years old. In all, 168 remains were found. There were also woven fabrics used to wrap the bodies for burial.

Brevard County, Map 5; trailoffloridasindianheritage.org/Brevard-museum-windover-pond; 5222 Windover Trail, Titusville, Florida, 32780; 321-632-1830.

YBOR CITY HISTORIC DISTRICT

Tampa

In the late 1800s, thousands of Cubans fled their island as revolutions brought turmoil between the Cubans and the Spanish, who controlled the island. Some settled in Key West and others went to New York, but many came to Tampa. Vicente Martinez Ybor once made cigars in Cuba, but his support for revolutionaries forced him to leave. He came to Tampa in 1885. Although his cigars were made in the United States, he used only Cuban tobacco and Cuban cigar makers. Soon, Tampa was known as the "Cigar Capital of the World." There were more than six thousand cigar workers in Tampa. Today, Ybor City has the largest collection of buildings related to the United States cigar industry and was a rare multiethnic and multiracial industrial community of the Deep South in the late nineteenth and early twentieth centuries. It was also a center for revolutionary activity, as the cigar makers made regular contributions to the efforts of Jose Marti to overthrow the Spanish. Most of the buildings in Ybor City were built between 1886 and World War I and include churches, social halls, restaurants, factories and public buildings. The place to start a tour is the Ybor City Chamber of Commerce Museum & Visitor Center at 1600 East 8th Avenue, 33605.

Hillsborough County, Map 7; ybor.org; 813-241-8838.

50 MUSEUMS

A.E. BACKUS GALLERY & MUSEUM

Fort Pierce

The A.E. Backus museum has had a strange fate. It is named for one of the state's leading artists, but it is his pupils who have gone on to enjoy worldwide fame. Backus was an artist as well as a teacher. As his fame grew, he found poor African American youths in Fort Pierce and taught them to paint landscapes. They proved to be apt pupils and began turning out paintings they sold for a few dollars. They came to be known as "the Highwaymen" because they often sold their work along the highways around Fort Pierce. The city opened a small museum for Backus, and some paintings by the Highwaymen were hung in a small back room. The city has spent millions expanding the museum and giving the Highwaymen the recognition they deserve. It is now the largest permanent display of Highwaymen art in the nation.

St. Lucie County, Map 4; backusmuseum.com; 500 North Indian River Drive, Fort Pierce, Florida, 34950; 772-465-0630.

AH-TAH-THI-KI MUSEUM

Clewiston

This museum is difficult to reach, located sixty miles west of Palm Beach, sixty miles east of Fort Myers and one hundred miles from Miami. The museum takes visitors back two centuries to tell the story of the Seminoles in Florida. *Ah-Tah-Thi-Ki* means "place of learning." When the United States acquired Florida, the Seminoles could be found throughout the state. The United States began a policy of Indian removal, forcing most of the Seminole tribe to head west. The Seminoles who remained fled to the Everglades and safety from soldiers. The museum is on the Big Cypress Seminole Indian Reservation and holds tens of thousands of artifacts telling the story of the tribe. Features include a one-mile boardwalk through the Everglades, Indian structures and special programs throughout the year. It is old Florida at its best.

Hendry County, Map 1; ahtahthiki.com; 34725 West Boundary Road, Clewiston, Florida, 33440; 877-902-1113.

ARCADIA MILL

Milton

Arcadia Mill was the first large water-powered industrial complex in Northwest Florida. It opened in the early nineteenth century and at its height had mills, shops, a horse-drawn railroad and a sixteen-mile log flume. Between 1817 and 1855, it processed tens of thousands of logs from the dense forests in the area. The Florida Department of State purchased much of the land and created an archaeological site. Those who study the site had little to go on. There were no drawings of the original site, and researchers have had to dig to find the history. Visitors can see the site; there is a visitor center and tours can be arranged.

Santa Rosa, Map 3; historicpensacola.org; 5709 Mill Pond Lane, Milton, Florida, 32583; 850-626-3084.

AUDUBON HOUSE AND TROPICAL GARDENS

Key West

Captain John Geiger built this sprawling home in the 1840s with the fortune he made in wrecking. It was common for ships to sink off the South Florida coast, and wreckers would salvage the ships and make a tidy profit. The

Early settlers to Florida recalled the skies darkening as thousands of birds flew overhead.
Many species of birds were all but eliminated by hunters and progress. John James
Audubon captured many of the birds during his journey through Florida.

Geiger family owned the home for a century, and by 1958, it was slated for demolition to make way for a gas station. At the time, Key West was much different than today, largely run-down, a village that went bankrupt during the Great Depression and faced an uncertain future. At the last minute, the house was saved and preserved as a beautiful home and gardens. The home was renamed the Audubon House in honor of John James Audubon, who visited the island in 1832. His artwork is featured inside the house.

Monroe County, Map 6; audubonhouse.com; 205 Whitehead Street, Key West, Florida, 33040; 305-294-2116.

BOCA EXPRESS TRAIN MUSEUM

Boca Raton

Boca Raton's 1930 Florida East Coast Railway Station has been preserved and is home to a pair of restored 1947 Seaboard Air Line streamlined rail cars. There is also a 1964 Atlantic Coast Line caboose and a 1930 Baldwin steam switch engine.

Palm Beach County, Map 4; bocahistory.org; 747 Dixie Highway, Boca Raton, Florida, 33432; 561-395-6766.

BRONSON-MULHOLLAND HOUSE

Palatka

During the 1850s, Palatka—or Pilatka, as it was then known—became a resort town as steamboats brought tourists up the St. Johns River. The Civil War nearly emptied the town, but when the war ended, the tourists returned. The town became a major railroad center and home to huge lumber mills. The Bronson-Mulholland House was built in 1854 by Judge Isaac Bronson. The house was occupied by Union troops during the Civil War and then became a school for freed slaves. In 1904, Mary Mulholland inherited the property, but she could not keep the large tract intact. She began selling lots to raise money. At her death, the mansion passed through a series of owners, and the house was divided into apartments. The house was rescued in 1965, when the city acquired it and began restoring it to its original glory.

Putnam County, Map 2; palatka-fl.gov; 100 Madison Street, Palatka, Florida, 32177; 386-329-0100.

BULOW PLANTATION RUINS HISTORIC STATE PARK

Flagler Beach

In the early 1800s, this was the largest plantation in East Florida, spanning nearly five thousand acres. Major Charles Bulow used his slaves to grow cotton, rice, indigo and sugarcane. In 1836, Seminole Indians attacked the plantation and destroyed much of it. The State of Florida acquired the property in 1945. The park is rich with bald eagles and manatees. There is a center with exhibits about the plantation.

Flagler County, Map 5; floridastateparks.org; 3501 Old Kings Road, Flagler Beach, Florida, 32136; 386-517-2084.

Not much remains of the once magnificent Bulow sugar works south of St. Augustine. But the state park around it has manatees and magnificent eagles, and there is an exhibit about plantation life.

CASA FELIZ HISTORIC HOME MUSEUM

Winter Park

In 1932, a wealthy Massachusetts industrialist asked the young architect James Gamble Rogers II to design a winter home in Winter Park. The industrialist gave Rogers freedom to design the house on the shores of Lake Osceola. The home was a landmark for seventy years, growing in fame as Rogers became one of the nation's best-known architects. In 2000, the house was sold, and the new owners planned to tear it down. The community of Winter Park rallied and raised $1.2 million to have it moved to open land nearby. The home was restored to its original condition and now is a showplace near downtown Winter Park.

Orange County, Map 5; casafeliz.us; 656 North Park Avenue, Winter Park, Florida, 32789; 407-628-8200.

CRACKER TRAIL MUSEUM

Zolfo Springs

The crackers were the early Florida pioneers. There are different versions about the origin of the name, but many believe that it came from the *crack* their whips made as they herded their cows. They were centered in Southwest Florida, although they drove their cows into Central Florida. In 1967, the Peace River Valley Historical Society started Pioneer Park in Zolfo Springs. There is an 1897 blacksmith shop, a 1914 Baldwin Locomotive and an 1879 cabin.

Hardee County, Map 1; hardeecounty.net; 2822 Museum Drive, Zolfo Springs, Florida, 33890; 863-473-5076.

DALÍ MUSEUM

St. Petersburg

In 1942, Reynolds and Eleanor Morse visited a Salvador Dalí exhibit in Cleveland and the following year purchased their first Dalí painting. Over the following four decades, they added to their collection and became friends with Dalí. In the 1970s, they decided to donate their huge collection of paintings, manuscripts, sculpture and books to a museum. It set off a contest. St. Petersburg rallied around the cause, and in 1982, the Dalí Museum opened. In 2011, a new building opened in downtown St. Petersburg.

Pinellas County, Map 7; thedali.org/visit/visitor-information; One Dali Boulevard, St. Petersburg, Florida, 33701.

DEBARY HALL HISTORIC SITE

DeBary

In 1871, Frederick deBary chose land on the St. Johns River to build his mansion. DeBary made his fortune as a wine merchant and spared no expense in building his home. He grew some oranges but primarily used his land for hunting and entertaining. In addition to the house, there is a stable and a visitor center.

Volusia County, Map 5; volusia.org; 198 Sunrise Boulevard, DeBary, Florida, 32713; 386-668-3840.

Frederick deBary, the champagne king, built the magnificent DeBary Hall on the banks of the St. Johns River.

DEERING ESTATE

Miami

Charles Deering was one of the wealthiest men in the nation in the 1920s as chairman and major stockholder in International Harvester Company. his sprawling mansion was surrounded by gardens and manicured grounds. After Deering's death, the estate passed to relatives, who were not interested in keeping it up, and the State of Florida took over. It is one of the nation's best examples of 1920s opulence, and visitors can enjoy the house and the many outside activities.

Miami-Dade County, Map 6; deeringestate.org; 16701 Southwest 72nd Avenue, Miami, Florida, 33157; 305-235-1668.

DE SOTO NATIONAL MEMORIAL

Bradenton

Hernando de Soto landed here in 1539 looking for wealth and glory. Instead, he found tragedy and death. He landed with 223 horses and 620 men, pets, food, servants and pigs. He landed in Charlotte Harbor and unloaded all his passengers and equipment. He traveled up the west coast, went east to present-day Lakeland and then swung back west and up to near present-day Tallahassee. They went to what is now Georgia and South Carolina and eventually ended on the banks of the Mississippi, where he died. The memorial is near Bradenton and sits on twenty-six acres of coastline and mangrove swamps. The Indian village Ucita has been reconstructed, and there are exhibits.

Manatee County, Map 1; nps.gov/deso; 8300 Desoto Memorial Highway, Bradenton, Florida, 34209; 941-792-0408 x105.

DOW MUSEUM OF HISTORIC HOUSES
St. Augustine

The nine houses that make up the Dow Museum were built between 1790 and 1910 and capture the history of the city. The exhibits include an archaeological record of a sixteenth-century hospital and cemetery, as well as a 1572 plan for St. Augustine. It was on this site that federal authorities read the 1863 Emancipation Proclamation, which freed the slaves in Florida. Stop by the General Store to see books about the history of St. Augustine.

St. Johns County, Map 2; visitstaugustine.com; 149 Cordova Street, St. Augustine, Florida, 32084; 904-823-9722.

EDISON AND FORD WINTER ESTATES

Fort Myers

When Thomas Edison came to Fort Myers in 1885, it was just a backwater village. He purchased thirteen acres on the Caloosahatchee River, and when he returned the following year, it was with his new bride. The family held the property for six decades. In 1947, his widow, Mina, gave the estate to the city. The result is that nearly all the furnishings belonged to the Edison family. Henry Ford first came to Fort Myers in 1914 when he visited Edison. Two years later, he purchased a home next to the Edison estate. The Fords sold the home at the end of World War II to a family who sold the house to the city in the late 1980s. The estate includes other buildings and shows how two of the richest men in the world lived.

Lee County, Map 1; edisonfordwinterestates.org; 2350 McGregor Boulevard, Fort Myers, Florida, 33901; 239-334-7419.

FLAGLER MUSEUM

Palm Beach

What was once described as a residence "more wonderful than any palace in Europe" was the home of Henry Flagler and his wife, Mary Kenan Flagler, from 1902 until his death in 1913. After it passed into private hands, it was turned into a hotel and came close to being razed in 1959. It was saved and converted into a magnificent museum.

Palm Beach County, Map 4; flaglermuseum.us; 1 Whitehall Way, Palm Beach, Florida, 33489; 561-655-2833.

Tallahassee was chosen as the capital because it was midway between the two early major cities, Pensacola and St. Augustine. The first capitol building was made of logs.

FLORIDA STATE CAPITOL

Tallahassee

By the 1970s, Florida had outgrown its capitol building and replaced it with what must be one of the ugliest capitol buildings in the nation. There were plans to tear down the 1902 capitol, but a preservation movement saved it; it has been restored to its 1902 state. It is a museum featuring displays centering on the state's political history.

Leon County, Map 3; flhistoriccapitol.gov; 400 South Monroe Street, Tallahassee, Florida, 32399; 850-487-1902.

FORT BARRANCAS

Pensacola

Today, the site of Fort Barrancas lies within the Naval Air Station Pensacola and overlooks Pensacola Bay. It was originally built by the Spanish as Fort San Carlos de Barrancas in 1787. It was rebuilt and expanded into brick. The army deactivated the fort in 1947 and eventually transferred it to the National Park Service. The fort was in an unusual situation during the Civil War. Union troops realized that Barrancas would be more difficult to defend than nearby Fort Pickens, and the soldiers were moved to Fort Pickens. Fort Barrancas was held by the Confederates, while Fort Pickens was held by the Union.

Escambia County, Map 3; nps.gov/guis; 3182 Taylor Road, Pensacola, Florida, 32508; 850-934-2600.

For a time, it appeared as though the Civil War might start in Pensacola as Confederate soldiers gathered at two forts.

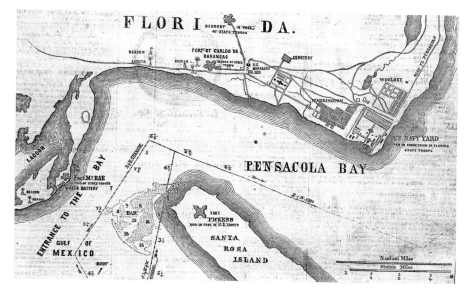

Pensacola has been a military center from the days of sailing ships to the jet age. During the Civil War, Union troops held Fort Pickens despite the presence of Confederate troops at Fort McRae and Fort Barrancas.

FORT CAROLINE NATIONAL MEMORIAL

Jacksonville

Briefly, the French tried to challenge Spain for control of Florida. In 1546, the French established a colony near present-day Jacksonville and built Fort Caroline. The settlers were French Huguenots, Protestants seeking religious freedom. The Spanish, who were responsible for spreading the Catholic faith, could not allow the Protestants to remain. They attacked the French, killing most of them. The land around Fort Caroline was also occupied by the Timucua Indians, who left behind artifacts. There is a visitor center and information about European exploration and settlement as well as the natives. There is a small replica of the French fort along with thousands of acres of pristine land.

Duval County, Map 2; nps.gov/timu; 12713 Fort Caroline Road, Jacksonville, Florida, 32225; 904-641-7155.

FORT CHRISTMAS HISTORICAL PARK

Orlando

Construction on the fort near Orlando began on Christmas Day 1837 as one of a series of forts to protect settlers and provide safety for soldiers during the Seminole War. At one time it was the base for two thousand soldiers. In the 1970s, the county government built a replica of the fort about a mile from the original site.

Orange County, Map 5; orangecountyfl.net/culturalparks; 1300 North Fort Christmas Road, Christmas, Florida, 32709; 407-254-9310.

FORT CLINCH STATE PARK

Fernandina Beach

Fort Clinch was one of the fortresses built in the mid-1800s and was the site of just one battle. In 1862, Union troops captured the fort from the Confederate soldiers who had seized it the previous year. It is much as it was in the 1800s and is a trip back in time. There is a visitor center, and military reenactments occur the first weekend of each month. There is also camping and wildlife in abundance.

Nassau County, Map 2; floridastateparks.org/fortclinch; 2601 Atlantic Avenue, Fernandina Beach, Florida, 32034; 905-277-7274.

FORT DE SOTO PARK

Tierra Verde

This park is made up of five keys, which were used for military fortifications, but today it is used for boating, picnics, hiking, cycling and kayaking. One of the area's main attractions is birdwatching. The area was occupied by the Tocobaga tribe about one thousand years ago. The Spanish under Pánfilo de Narváez came in 1529, and a decade later, Hernando de Soto arrived on his journey throughout the United States. The U.S. Army engineers arrived in 1849, including future Confederate general Robert E. Lee. Union troops were stationed there during the Civil War to blockade Tampa Bay. Fortifications were built for the Spanish-American War, and one of the keys was used by the Marine Hospital Service as a quarantine station. Fort De Soto construction began in 1898 and was completed in 1906. The sprawling fort closed in 1910, and most of the troops were moved to Alabama. It saw service again in World War II and then was acquired by Pinellas County for use as a park.

Pinellas County, Map 7; pinellascounty.org/parks; 3500 Pinellas Bayway South, Tierra Verde, Florida, 33715; 727-582-2100.

FORT FOSTER STATE HISTORIC SITE

Zephyrhills

This is one of the forts erected during the Seminole War, built in 1836 but soon destroyed. It was rebuilt later that year with two blockhouses and a wooden encampment. The fort's main purpose was to supply soldiers fighting Seminoles in the area. Disease forced the fort to close in 1837, but it saw service again later in the year. The fort opened and closed as problems with the Seminoles flared. A replica of the fort was built in 1980.

Pasco County, Map 7; floridastateparks.org; 15402 US-301, Zephyrhills, Florida, 33592; 813-987-6771.

FORT MATANZAS NATIONAL MONUMENT

St. Augustine

A few miles north, the sprawling Fort San Marcos draws hundreds of thousands of visitors a year to St. Augustine. But Fort Matanzas may be more intriguing than its larger and more popular neighbor. Fort Matanzas is on an island that can be reached only by a small boat (provided without charge by the National Park Service). Fort Matanzas was built as a lookout fort for the larger fort fifteen miles away. Built by the Spanish in 1742, it

Although it is far less known than the sprawling Fort San Marcos a few miles north, Fort Matanzas is a great adventure. Located on a tiny island, it can be reached by a boat provided by the National Park Service.

protects Matanzas Inlet. The name of the inlet and the fort comes from the executions of the French carried out by the Spanish in 1565. *Matanzas* is Spanish for "slaughter."

St. Johns County, Map 2; nps.gov/foma; 8635 A1A South, St. Augustine, Florida, 32080; 904-471-0116.

FORT MOSE HISTORIC STATE PARK

St. Augustine

The site of Fort Mose has some of the most dramatic history in Florida. In 1738, the Spanish governor ordered a fort built for a free black settlement—the first in what became the United States. Spain offered asylum to slaves from the British colonies if they converted to Catholicism. Arming the freed slaves created a line of defense north of St. Augustine, and it damaged the economy of South Carolina and Georgia by hurting the plantation labor supply. The fort was destroyed in a fight with the British in 1740 but rebuilt a decade later. In 1763, the British took control of Florida, and most of the free black inhabitants migrated to Cuba. The original fort is gone, but there are displays and a visitor center that explains the importance of the fort.

St. Johns County, Map 2; floridastateparks.org; 15 Fort Mose Trail, St. Augustine, Florida; 904-823-2232.

FORT ZACHARY TAYLOR HISTORIC STATE PARK

Key West

Fort Zachary Taylor is on the southern edge of Key West and is one of the sprawling brick forts built in Florida before the Civil War. Despite its strategic location, it was never used in war, although it continues to be home to the largest cache of Civil War weapons in the world. The fort was heavily armed during the Civil War and the Spanish-American War, and the Civil War guns are on display.

Monroe County, Map 6; floridastateparks.org; 601 Howard England Way, Key West, Florida, 33040; 305-292-6713.

FOUNTAIN OF YOUTH ARCHAEOLOGICAL PARK

St. Augustine

This is a strange site. In 1904, a woman named Luella Day McConnell arrived in St. Augustine and soon was telling residents that a fourteen-acre site she owned was the landing place of Juan Ponce de León when he discovered Florida. She embellished the story with false evidence but was able to convince millions of Americans that she owned the true Fountain of Youth. She created a major tourist attraction, even though her claims were false. It might have remained just a tourist attraction with a dubious claim if a gardener planting trees had not found a skeleton in 1934. The remains turned out to be an aboriginal Native American. Research by the Smithsonian Institution found that the area was the burial place of more than four thousand Native Americans. The site also yielded the location of the 1587 Franciscan Mission of Nombre de Dios, the first Christian mission in what became the United States. More than eighty years of excavations have caused historians to reassess their views of early American history. McConnell's tourist creation turned out to have tremendous significance. Visitors can see the historical site and drink from what McConnell claimed was the Fountain of Youth.

St. Johns County, Map 2; fountainofyouthflorida.com; 11 Magnolia Avenue, St. Augustine, Florida, 32084; 904-829-3168.

GAMBLE PLANTATION HISTORIC STATE PARK

Ellenton

Major Robert Gamble once owned 3,500 acres and nearly two hundred slaves to work them, growing sugarcane south of St. Petersburg. Maintaining the large plantation caused Gamble to go into debt, and in 1856, he was forced to sell. Captain Archibald McNeill, a Confederate blockade runner, moved in during the Civil War, although the sugar mill was destroyed by Union soldiers in 1864. The ruins still stand. The plantation had its brush with history in 1865 when Judah P. Benjamin came by. Benjamin served in the Confederate cabinet and was one of President Jefferson Davis's closest aides. With the Confederacy collapsing, Davis and his aides fled Richmond and slowly made their way south. Davis was captured in Georgia just as he was about to enter Florida. Benjamin continued south, heading down the west coast of Florida. He stopped at the Gamble mansion before moving on down to Cuba and eventually to England. As the other plantation mansions in the area fell into disrepair or were abandoned, the Gamble Mansion remained, although by 1902, it also was in poor condition. In 1925, the United Daughters of the Confederacy purchased the home and saved it from almost certain destruction. The group donated the site to the State of Florida, which keeps it much as it was in the mid-1850s.

Manatee County, Map 1; floridastateparks.org/parks; 3708 Patten Avenue, Ellenton, Florida, 34222; 941-723-4536.

GOVERNMENT HOUSE MUSEUM

St. Augustine

Government House is located on the plaza in downtown St. Augustine. The Spanish king decreed that every town in the New World contain a plaza for the government, church and public. The building in St. Augustine was built in 1598, just eight years after the Spanish arrived. The building passed to British control in 1763 and then back to Spain in 1783. When the United States acquired Florida, the building was used as a courthouse and later the capital of the Florida territory. In 1836, the building underwent "renovation," which involved removing a five-story tower and a porch. In

1937, there was another renovation, this time turning it into a post office and customs house. The state acquired the building and renovated it again. Today, it is administered by the University of Florida. The house is open to the public, and there are exhibits about the history of St. Augustine.

St. Johns County, Map 2; staugustine.ufl.edu; 48 King Street, St. Augustine, Florida, 32084; 904-825-5034.

HISTORIC HAILE HOMESTEAD AT KANAPAHA PLANTATION
Gainesville

In 1854, Thomas Evans Haile and his family came to Alachua County to establish a 1,500-acre cotton plantation. He built a 6,200-square-foot home. The house passed to one of their fifteen children, Evans, an attorney who began an unusual legacy. Guests wrote on the walls, including lists of partygoers at the home. In all, the walls contain thousands of words and are known as "The Talking Walls." By the 1930s, the mansion had been abandoned and boarded up. It remained that way until the 1970s, when director Victor Nunez used it to film his movie *Gal Young 'Un*. He fell in love with the home, and it led to efforts by the state to restore the home in 1996.

Alachua County, Map 2; hailehomestead.org; 8500 Southwest Archer Road, Gainesville, Florida, 32608; 352-336-9096.

HISTORIC PLANTATION VILLAGE
Pensacola

Next to St. Augustine, Pensacola has Florida's most historic downtown. The historic area covers about eight acres and includes twenty-eight properties within what were the Spanish and British forts. The Spanish came first, founded by Spanish sailor Tristán de Luna y Arellano in 1559. Pensacola and St. Augustine battled over which city was the first European settlement in North America. A visitor can see it all with a walking tour.

Escambia County, Map 3; visitpensacola.com; 205 Zaragoza Street, Pensacola, Florida, 32502; 850-595-5990.

HISTORYMIAMI

Miami

HistoryMiami is the museum of Miami, dedicated to finding and preserving the area's rich heritage. There are regular exhibits and programs and tours by the city's leading historian, Paul George. It is the largest museum in Florida and the most ambitious. It is home to the annual Miami International Map Fair, the largest of its kind in the Western Hemisphere. HistoryMiami dates back to 1940, when it was founded as the Historical Museum of Southern Florida. Exhibits include a 1920s trolley car, booty from shipwrecks and rafts that brought Cuban refugees to Florida.

Miami-Dade County, Map 6; historymiami.org; 101 West Flagler Street, Miami, Florida, 33130; 305-375-1492.

JEWISH MUSEUM OF FLORIDA

Miami

Located in two restored former synagogues in downtown Miami, the museum focuses on Jewish life in Florida. The first synagogue in Miami was built in 1929. The very location of the synagogue has a tragic history. The location was selected because at the time it was one of the few neighborhoods where Jews could live in Miami. Earlier, Jews had been denied permission to build a synagogue in the city. They had to take a ferry across Biscayne Bay to pray. In 1924, one Jewish group was holding services in a vacant lot on Washington Avenue, and services were also held in an apartment building on Collins Avenue. As other synagogues were built and members moved from their neighborhood, the membership dwindled. The museum holds more than 100,000 objects, including photographs, documents and religious objects related to Jewish heritage in the state.

Miami-Dade County, Map 6; jmof.fiu.edu; 301 Washington Avenue, Miami Beach, Florida, 33139; 305-672-5044.

RICHARD AND PAT JOHNSON PALM BEACH COUNTY HISTORY MUSEUM

West Palm Beach

In 1937, the Historical Society of Palm Beach County was formed, and although its collections grew, it became something of a vagabond, wandering through half a dozen locations before finding a permanent home in the county's 1916 courthouse. The museum has put many of its holdings online, and there are special exhibits throughout the year.

Palm Beach County, Map 4; hspbc.org; 300 North Dixie Highway, West Palm Beach, Florida, 33401; 561-832-4164.

KINGSLEY PLANTATION

Jacksonville

Zephaniah Kingsley spent twenty-five years building his plantation on the tip of Fort George Island. He eventually owned one thousand acres. The site combines two entirely different histories. Long before Kingsley arrived, the site was occupied by the Timucuas and has become a major preserve. There are also the remains of a Spanish mission.

Duval County, Map 2; nps.gov/timu; 11676 Palmetto Avenue, Jacksonville, Florida, 32226; 904-641-7155.

KORESHAN STATE HISTORIC SITE

Estero

During the 1800s, Florida attracted religious sects such as the Shakers and Koreshan Unity. The Koreshan site in Southwest Florida dates from 1893, when the Koreshans built a settlement based on the idea that the universe exists inside the earth. The members lived celibate lives and farmed and planted botanical gardens. The site has eleven restored buildings and remains as tranquil as it was more than a century ago. The sect's members declined, and the property was turned over to the state in 1961.

Lee County, Map 1; floridastateparks.org; 3800 Corkscrew Road, Estero, Florida, 33928; 239-992-0311.

MANATEE VILLAGE HISTORICAL PARK

Bradenton

Step back in history to see what the Bradenton area was like from 1840 to 1920. Start with the 1903 Wiggins General Store, which served the village of Manatee on the first floor and was a boardinghouse on the second floor. King Wiggins had the only store for miles around, and often people would spend the day traveling to his store and spend the night before heading home with their purchases. The boat works shows how Captain Bat Fogarty built boats more than a century ago. There is a blacksmith shop and a typical settler's house. Florida cattlemen called their hands cow hunters rather than cowboys. The museum features a two-story cow hunters' bunkhouse, a temporary shelter used on the range to house cow hunters as they rounded up the herd.

Manatee County, Map 1; manateevillage.org; 1404 Manatee Avenue East, Bradenton, Florida, 34208; 941-749-7165.

MEL FISHER MARITIME HERITAGE MUSEUM

Key West

The name links this site to famed treasure hunter Mel Fisher, but the museum is much more than that. There are artifacts from multiple seventeenth-century shipwrecks, including the *Santa Margarita* and the *Henrietta Marie*. There are even artifacts from the *Santa Clara*, which went down in 1564. There are exhibits on a variety of subjects and a laboratory for research. Visitors can touch artifacts and learn about preservation, making the museum unusual. It is one of Key West's real treasures.

Monroe County, Map 6; melfisher.org; 1322 US-1, Sebastian, Florida, 32958; 305-294-2633.

MUSEUM OF FLORIDA HISTORY
Tallahassee

Florida has a fascinating and unique history. Founded by the Spanish, Florida has a history far different from the British colonies to the north. The museum starts with the dinosaurs and goes to the present day. There is a twelve-thousand-year-old mastodon skeleton from Wakulla Springs, Indian canoes and coins from Spanish shipwrecks. The museum also controls the nearby Knott House, which was the headquarters for Union troops who occupied the city at the end of the Civil War. From its steps, the Emancipation Proclamation was read, proclaiming freedom for the slaves. Later, it was used as an office by the state's first black physician.

Leon County, Map 3; museumofloridahistory.com; 500 South Bronough Street, Tallahassee, Florida, 32399; 850-245-6400.

NORMAN STUDIOS SILENT FILM MUSEUM
Jacksonville

One of the little-known chapters of the moviemaking industry is a stop in Jacksonville. In the early 1900s, the movie industry came to Northeast Florida and produced hundreds of films. The moviemakers were escaping from Thomas Edison and New York. In Florida, they found new surroundings to film and weather that made moviemaking possible year-round, avoiding the tight control of Edison. Eventually, there were some thirty movie studios, including Eagle Studios. Eagle sold out to Norman Laboratories with a new target audience. Richard Norman aimed his movies at African American audiences. Of all the studios, the Norman buildings were the only ones to survive, and the five buildings where the movies were made have been preserved.

Duval County, Map 2; normanstudios.org; 6337 Arlington Road, Jacksonville, Florida, 32211; 904-742-7011.

ORANGE COUNTY REGIONAL HISTORY CENTER

Orlando

Located in the old courthouse in the center of Orlando, the museum has a huge collection of Central Florida photographs and memorabilia. The museum holds a large collection related to the tragic 2016 shooting at the Pulse nightclub that left forty-nine people dead. There are regular speakers and other programs, which make it the cultural center for Orange County.

Orange County, Map 5; thehistorycenter.org; 65 East Central Boulevard, Orlando, Florida, 32801; 407-836-8500.

PAYNES CREEK HISTORIC STATE PARK

Bowling Green

This park has a tragic history. When the Second Seminole War ended in 1842, the Seminoles were given a reservation in Southwest Florida. Settlers ignored the rights of the Indians and began claiming land. In 1849, the Indians killed two men who operated a trading post and burned their store. Settlers fled, and the U.S. government built Fort Chokonikla to protect the settlers. The fort could protect the settlers but not the soldiers, who succumbed to malaria. Less than a year after it opened, the fort was closed. Today, it is a wilderness with canoeing, fishing and kayaking. There is a visitor center showing what life was like more than a century ago.

Hardee County, Map 1; floridastateparks.org; 888 Lake Branch Road, Bowling Green, Florida, 33834; 863-375-4717.

THE RINGLING

Sarasota

The circus king John Ringling made Sarasota the winter home of his circus and built one of the most beautiful homes in the United States. He

Circus king John Ringling built the most magnificent mansion in Florida, with works of art from all over the world.

first went there in 1911 and purchased twenty acres. He kept buying until he owned 25 percent of the property in the town. He spent $1.5 million to build a five-story mansion covering thirty-six thousand square feet. He called it Ca' d'Zan and brought back artwork and books from Europe. His collection became so large that he built a museum for his treasures.

The estate as a whole is named The Ringling. In 2000, control passed to Florida State University. It is one of the most eclectic collections in the world, in a magnificent setting.

Sarasota County, Map 1; ringling.org; 5401 Bay Shore Road, Sarasota, Florida, 34243; 941-359-5700.

SAN MARCOS DE APALACHE HISTORIC STATE PARK

St. Marks

San Marcos began as a Spanish fort on the Gulf Coast in the late 1600s. The original fort made of wood was destroyed by a violent storm, which drowned the soldiers inside. It was replaced with a stone structure in the mid-1700s. The British took over the fort a decade later; the Spanish returned, and the United States took the fort in 1821. The Confederacy held the fort during the Civil War, adding a hospital. At the end of the Civil War, the fort was abandoned. Today, there are remains of the stone fort, and a visitor center traces the history of the fort.

Wakulla County, Map 1; floridastateparks.org; 148 Old Fort Road, St. Marks, Florida, 32355; 850-922-6007.

SOCIETY OF THE FOUR ARTS

Palm Beach

This is one of the most beautiful museums in Florida, located among the enclave of Palm Beach. It is difficult to describe the museum, which offers a bit of everything, including an art gallery, gardens, a library, concerts, films and distinguished speakers. It was founded in 1936 to offer cultural programs for the growing Palm Beach community and eventually expanded to fill a magnificent campus.

Palm Beach, Map 4; fourarts.org; 100 Four Arts Plaza, Palm Beach, Florida, 33480; 561-655-7227.

ST. AUGUSTINE LIGHTHOUSE & MARITIME MUSEUM

St. Augustine

For 450 years, there has been a watch along the coast of Florida. Beginning with the Spanish, the effort to aid navigation survived under four flags. At first, there were wooden watchtowers with a flame to warn approaching ships. In 1824, three years after the United States acquired Florida, an existing coquina structure became a lighthouse, which was used until a new lighthouse was built in 1871. The lights went on in 1874 but lasted just six years before failing in a storm. The current lighthouse was built near a house of the light keeper. The lighthouse and the keeper's house have been restored, and visitors can climb the 219 steps to the top; for one dollar you can purchase a certificate proving your accomplishment.

St. Johns County, Map 2; staugustinelighthouse.com; 81 Lighthouse Avenue, St. Augustine, Florida, 32080; 904-829-0745.

STEPHEN FOSTER FOLK CULTURE CENTER STATE PARK

White Springs

Originally, Stephen Foster's song included the lyrics, "Way down upon the Pee Dee River," a reference to a river in South Carolina. He changed it to, "Way down upon the Suwannee River," and Florida got a state song. The eight-hundred-acre state park is on the banks of the Suwannee—Foster never saw the river or Florida—and includes exhibits about Foster's life and a ninety-seven-bell carillon that plays Foster's songs. There are displays of blacksmithing, stained glass making and camping. There is also canoeing and hiking, and over the Memorial Day weekend, it is home to the Florida Folk Festival.

Hamilton County, Map 2; floridastateparks.org; 11016 Lillian Sanders Drive, White Springs, Florida, 32096; 386-397-4331.

TALLAHASSEE MUSEUM

Tallahassee

The Tallahassee Museum is a mix of nature and history. The Tallahassee Junior Museum is aimed at schoolchildren. For those looking for history, there is the Bellevue plantation house, the Bethlehem Missionary Baptist Church, a classic train caboose and an old schoolhouse. The grounds are much as they were more than a century ago. There is a farm with displays of quilting, gardening, blacksmithing and cooking. There is even a zipline for the adventurous.

Leon County, Map 3; tallahasseemuseum.org; 3945 Museum Road, Tallahassee, Florida, 32310; 850-575-8684.

TRUMAN WHITE HOUSE

Key West

Harry Truman had a problem: he had very little money. Unlike today's presidents, who often take lavish vacations, Truman usually went home to Independence, Missouri, for his vacations while he was in the Senate and as vice president. As president, he found the perfect vacation spot—at no cost. He could stay at the navy base in Key West. He fell in love with the place, and during his eight years as president, he spent a total of eight months at Key West in eleven visits. His visits were so frequent that it became known as the Little White House. The Key West Submarine Base, along with the Little White House, were closed in 1974, but as Truman's reputation improved, money was raised to restore the Little White House, which is now owned by the State of Florida but run by a foundation.

Monroe County, Map 6; trumanlittlewhitehouse.com; 111 Front Street, Key West, Florida, 33040; 305-294-9911.

T.T. WENTWORTH JR. FLORIDA STATE MUSEUM

Pensacola

The museum started as a roadside stand in the suburb of Ensley more than sixty years ago, operated by T.T. Wentworth, who collected items that piqued his interest. In 1980, he offered to donate his collection to the City of Pensacola if a permanent home could be found. The city offered its old city hall. The collection is in downtown Pensacola within walking distance of many of the city's historical sites. The collection defies a simple description and includes a mummified cat. There is even an interactive science museum, along with city artifacts. Be sure to see the collection of Blue Angel memorabilia.

Escambia County, Map 3; 330 South Jefferson Street, Pensacola, Florida, 32502; 850-595-5990.

25 WRITERS

JOHN JAMES AUDUBON

Key West

Audubon first came to Florida in 1831, visiting St. Augustine, where he painted birds, but he hated the city, its residents and the alligators—he worried they would eat his dog. He gave up on Florida after just a few months but returned in 1832 after hearing that Key West had scores of bird species. He stayed at 205 Whitehead Street and found several rare breeds, including the white-crowned pigeon. Audubon said, "Seldom have I experienced greater pleasures than when on the Florida Keys." His trip was such a success that he planned a third trip but canceled it because of the outbreak of the Second Seminole War. He later returned to Pensacola but could not arrange transportation for further travel. Much of his work appeared in *The Birds of America*. He also wrote the short story "Death of a Pirate," which is based on a true story.

The Audubon House at 205 Whitehead Street is open daily with tours. In addition to the magnificent house, there are lush gardens and antique furniture.

JOHN MUIR

Cedar Key

In 1867, John Muir began a walk from Indiana to Florida. He walked for nearly seven weeks before writing in his diary, "Today, at last, I reached Florida." He stopped at Fernandina Beach and then moved through Gainesville. He reached his goal, Cedar Key, and found a booming town. It was the wooden pencil capital of the world. Eberhard Faber and the Eagle Pencil Company both built mills in Cedar Key to take advantage of the wood. Muir took a job in a local sawmill, where he contracted malaria. His dream of eventually walking to South America came to an end, and Cedar Key became the end of his walk. He recorded his travels in his book *A Thousand-Mile Walk to the Gulf.*

Muir's travels are commemorated in a number of places. There is a historic marker in Cedar Key, and the John Muir Ecological Park is located in Yulee near Fernandina Beach. The park was the spot where the railroad bed began that Muir used for his famous walk across Florida. The Cedar Key Museum State Park (floridastateparks.org/parks-and-trails/cedar-key-museum-state-park) features displays about Muir's travels and his time in Cedar Key.

HARRIET BEECHER STOWE

Jacksonville

At the start of the Civil War, Harriet Beecher Stowe was one of the best-known authors in the nation. Her book *Uncle Tom's Cabin* stirred the nation and helped increase antislavery feelings in the North. After the war, she moved to Jacksonville to help her son and the newly freed slaves. Her son, Frederick, was an alcoholic, and she thought that a change of scenery would help him. She purchased a former plantation for Frederick at Mandarin, but as he had done throughout his life, he failed. He left Florida and set out for California, where he vanished. She remained in a home on the banks of the St. Johns, returned to writing and ran a school for former slaves. Her home became a tourist attraction, and she sat on her front

Harriet Beecher Stowe often sat on the banks outside her home on the St. Johns as the steamboats passed. She became a major tourist attraction.

porch as the steamboats full of tourists passed. She became so popular that she built a large dock in front of her house for ships. She became a major tourist attraction and wrote a column about Florida that became a book, *Palmetto Leaves*. The book helped promote Florida tourism and gave advice for purchasing land. The house is gone, but one of the buildings she built still stands; there is now a museum on the site.

The Mandarin Museum (mandarinmuseum.net) features displays about Stowe and her life in Florida. It is located at 12471 Mandarin Road in Jacksonville. It is open Saturdays.

JOHN GREENLEAF WHITTIER

Pensacola

John Greenleaf Whittier never set foot in Florida, but his writing about an incident in Florida raised antislavery fever in the North. Whittier's writings of a brutal incident angered many Americans. His poem told the story of Captain Jonathan Walker, who helped slaves escape from Pensacola. Search parties tracked them down, and they were taken to Key West, where Walker was arrested. Walker was returned to Pensacola, where he was held in jail for several months before a federal court found him guilty of slave stealing. In addition to a fine, he was sentenced to be placed in stocks and pelted with eggs and fruit and then taken to the courtroom, where the letters "S S," for slave stealer, were branded into his palm. The cruelty of his sentence made him a hero in the North and led Whittier to write the poem "The Branded Hand."

FREDERIC REMINGTON

Arcadia

When people think of the frontier, they think of the far West. But the last frontier in the continental United States was Southwest Florida, site of the last cattle drives and the last gunfights over rustling. Frederic Remington had captured the West in both paintings and sculpture, and in 1895, *Harper's Weekly* sent him to Southwest Florida to make a series of drawings of the

Author and artist Frederic Remington became famous for capturing the settlers in the West. He went to Southwest Florida to capture the cattle drives and rustlers for *Harper's Weekly*.

Florida cowboys and write about their lives. His article "Cracker Cowboys of Florida" found the Florida cowboys like those in the West, although he was unimpressed with both their horses and the cows.

JULES VERNE

Tampa

Jules Verne never visited Florida, but his ability to see the future for the state was uncanny. In the 1860s, Verne wrote *From the Earth to the Moon*, and a century later, his predictions came true. For his book, he did extensive research on Florida and wrote of a moon launch from Tampa—about 120 miles from the true site of the launch one hundred years later. In Verne's book, there were three crew members—just as in the Apollo flights. In the book, the spacecraft is named *Columbiad*—the Apollo craft was named

Columbia. In both the book and real life, the craft splashes down in the Pacific and is picked up by the U.S. Navy. As Apollo 11 returned to Earth from its moon landing, Neil Armstrong said, "A hundred years ago, Jules Verne wrote a book about a voyage to the Moon."

JAMES WELDON JOHNSON

Jacksonville

James Weldon Johnson grew up in Jacksonville, where he wrote what is considered the "Black national anthem."

James Weldon Johnson emerged as one of the early civil rights pioneers as newspaper publisher, teacher, principal, poet and first African American president of the NAACP. He and his brother wrote the poem "Lift Every Voice and Sing," which was adopted by the NAACP as the "Black national anthem." He also wrote the novel *The Autobiography of an Ex-Colored Man.* His birth site is now a park near the Prime Osborn Convention Center. The small frame house he grew up in was torn down long ago.

STEPHEN CRANE

Jacksonville

Crane came to Florida on his way to report on the growing problems in Cuba that led to the Spanish-American War. Crane arrived in Jacksonville to look for a ship to take him to Cuba. He was one of the best-known American writers because of his book *The Red Badge of Courage.* He used the alias "Samuel Carleton" so that he would not be bothered by fans. He found a ship, the *Commodore,* but as they set sail, the ship struck a sandbar. Once off the sandbar, they encountered a violent storm, and he nearly died. The ship sank, and Crane made it to shore near Daytona Beach. Crane turned his exploits into one of his best-selling works, *The Open Boat.* The Lilian Place Heritage Center (lilianplacehc.org) in Daytona Beach is where Crane spent the night after being saved. It was built in 1884 and is the oldest home on the beachside of Daytona Beach. It is open Wednesday through Monday in the afternoon. The Ponce de León Inlet Lighthouse (ponceinlet.org) is an excellent source of information about the *Commodore*, and Lead Docent John Mann has developed a following for his portrayal of the captain of the ship.

DAMON RUNYON

Miami

Damon Runyon was one of the best-known writers in the early 1900s. He was also one of the most successful. He wrote for the *New York American*, and it was Runyon who nicknamed boxer James J. Braddock "Cinderella Man," which would later be used as the title of a movie about Braddock. Runyon first came to Miami in the 1920s and found a wide-open town, with gambling, drinking and shady characters all around. One of his best friends was Al Capone. He and his young wife built a beautiful home on Hibiscus Island off Miami. Words he coined became part of the language—in Runyon's stories, head became "noggin," a knife was a "shiv," a hand grenade was a "pineapple" and a handgun was a "roscoe." He was a heavy smoker, and in 1944, his voice box was removed. His wife left him for a younger man, and

Writer Damon Runyon bought this Miami home for his new wife. Even though she divorced him for a much younger man, she ended up with the home on Hibiscus Island after a dispute over his will.

he died in 1946, thinking about his former wife and the Miami house. Even though she had left him, he included her in his will, leaving her the mansion and an interest in his writing. One of his short stories he left her became the play and movie *Guys and Dolls*.

The Runyon home is located on Hibiscus Island located off the MacArthur Causeway between Miami and Miami Beach.

ZORA NEALE HURSTON

Fort Pierce

Zora Neale Hurston grew up in Eatonville, a small town outside Orlando. She was working as a maid when the white woman she was working for saw her potential and arranged for her to finish high school and go to college. She was in New York as the Harlem Renaissance began and wrote stories while studying at Columbia University. Back in Florida, she wrote *Mules and Men* while living in Eau Gallie. Later, she wrote *Their Eyes Were Watching God* and taught at Bethune-Cookman University. But her writing fell out of favor, and she went from job to job, always moving down the economic ladder. She ended up in Fort Pierce working as a maid, but mostly trying to survive. In 1958, she suffered a series of strokes and was admitted to the St. Lucie County Welfare Home, where she died in 1960, alone and forgotten.

Zora Neale Hurston grew up in Eatonville and achieved fame before dying in poverty in Fort Pierce.

In Fort Pierce, one of Hurston's final homes at 809 North Ninth Street is a museum. There is a second Hurston home at 1734 Avenue L. The Zora Neale Hurston Dust Tracks Heritage Trail celebrates her final years in Fort Pierce. It features eight sites related to Zora. (Go to cityoffortpierce.com/386/Zora-Neale-Hurston-Dust-Tracks-Heritage.)

ERNEST HEMINGWAY

Key West

Ernest Hemingway came to Key West for a car and stayed for decades. He was on his way from Cuba to the United States when his wife's wealthy uncle purchased a car for the couple and told them they could stop in Key West and pick it up. When they arrived in Key West, an apologetic Ford dealer told them there was a delay, but to soothe one of the world's most famous authors, he put the couple up until the car arrived. It took two weeks, and during that time, Hemingway fell in love with the island. The couple purchased one of the largest houses on the island, and Hemingway became a major tourist attraction. People flocked to his home hoping for a glimpse or perhaps an autograph. At one point, Hemingway went into a favorite bar, and the bartender asked if he wanted to settle his previous tab. He denied running up a tab and found that a lookalike was using his name and charging things. Instead of being angry, Hemingway hired the man to hang around his house, sign autographs and shake hands. Thousands of people went away thinking they had met the real Hemingway When he went fishing with the author John Dos Passos, Hemingway tried to shoot a shark with his rifle, but the bullet struck the boat, bounced back and struck him in the leg. In late 1936, he met journalist Martha Gelhorn at Sloppy Joe's Bar and began an affair. He divorced his wife, who got the Key West home. After that, Hemingway was an infrequent visitor to Key West.

He first stayed at the Trev-Mor Hotel above the auto dealership at 314 Simonton Street. It is now a private residence. The Hemingway House is at 907 Whitehead Street. The home is open daily from 9:00 a.m. to 5:00 p.m. No trip to learn about Hemingway would be complete without a trip to Sloppy Joe's. The original was at 428 Greene Street, but Joe Russell moved his bar to its present location at 201 Duval Street. Hemingway spent most of his time at the original site and met his future wife there. But he spent lots of time in both bars.

JOHN KENNEDY

Palm Beach

When Joseph Kennedy purchased a mansion in Palm Beach in 1933, John F. Kennedy was a student at the boarding school Choate. Unlike his younger siblings, he was an infrequent visitor to Palm Beach. After Choate, he went to Harvard and then entered World War II. Throughout his life, he suffered serious health problems, and pain in his back was only aggravated by his activities during the war. After the war, Kennedy traveled to Palm Beach to recuperate from surgeries. In 1954, he underwent back surgery and began work on the Pulitzer Prize–winning book *Profiles in Courage*. For more than half a century, the true authorship of the book remained controversial. Finally, in 2008, his speechwriter, Ted Sorensen, revealed that while Kennedy conceived the book and wrote the first and last chapters, it was Sorensen who wrote most of the book. Kennedy and Sorensen also worked on Kennedy's best-known work, his 1961 inaugural address with the famous line, "Ask not what your country can do for you; but what you can do for your country." The Kennedy family sold the house in the 1990s. The home is located at 1095 North Ocean Boulevard in Palm Beach.

JAMES MERRILL

Key West

James Merrill was born into a life of privilege, the son of the Merrill in Merrill Lynch & Company, the New York stock brokerage. In 1950, Merrill met David Jackson, who became his partner for nearly three decades. All of Merrill's grandparents were born in North Florida, and he loved what he called old Florida. "This for me, accordingly, represents the 'real' Florida, as distinguished from the geriatric or economic ghettos proliferating to the South." He and Jackson began spending winters in Key West, and in 1982, they purchased a home on Elizabeth Street at the top of Solares Hill, the highest point on the island. Key West reminded him of what Florida once was. "Key West, when I first began to winter there struck me as preserving a touch or two of that original innocence: great trees, cracked sidewalks, the sociable cemetery. I hope

I disappear before they do." In his first years in Key West, it was perfect, but gradually, Merrill began to allow shady characters and lovers into his home. He died of complications from AIDS in 1995.

Merrill's house is at 702 Elizabeth Street and has an unusual history. It was built in the Bahamas and moved by barge to Key West.

TENNESSEE WILLIAMS

Key West

Tennessee Williams first came to Florida in 1939, working as a telegraph operator—one of his many failed careers. A few years later, he fled to Key West after his play *Band of Angels* opened to disastrous reviews. He lived in a small cabin, used by slaves eighty years earlier. "I am occupying the old servants' quarters in back of this 90-year-old house. It has been converted into an attractive living space with a shower. The rent is $7 a week." In 1942, with World War II underway, he went to work as a message decoder in Jacksonville. One night, he overlooked an important message and was fired. When he

As Tennessee Williams achieved greater success, his living conditions in Key West improved. This was his home for thirty-four years.

Even though *The Rose Tattoo* takes place in New Orleans, author Tennessee Williams insisted that the movie version be filmed in Key West. The movie won three Academy Awards.

returned to Key West after the war, he was famous. His play *The Glass Menagerie* was a hit on Broadway. Ernest Hemingway was spending less and less time on the island, and Williams emerged as the island's leading writer. He moved into a cottage, entertaining such writers as Carson McCullers, Gore Vidal and Christopher Isherwood. While staying in a nearby hotel, he completed *Summer and Smoke*. He made enough money from *A Streetcar Named Desire* and *The Glass Menagerie* to purchase a home at 1431 Duncan Street. There, he wrote *Night of the Iguana*. The movie version of his play *The Rose Tattoo* was filmed on the island and won three Academy Awards. His gay lifestyle was accepted by most Key West residents, but not all. One night, he was leaving a gay club with writer Dotson Rader when he was attacked by four or five men. Still, he remained on the island. He wanted to be buried at sea off Key West, but his brother buried him in St. Louis.

ÁLVAR NÚNEZ CABEZA DE VACA

The first book published about what would become the United States was written by a Spanish explorer decades before settlers arrived at Jamestown or Plymouth Rock. It became the first major account of life in North America. Álvar Núnez Cabeza de Vaca sailed for Florida in 1527 with an expedition of six hundred men with plans to settle on the Gulf Coast of Florida. The expedition was a disaster. There were storms, desertions and arguments, and in the end, only a handful survived. De Vaca went looking for help, unsure of exactly where other Spaniards might be. He sailed across the Gulf of Mexico and landed in Galveston. He wandered around the Southwest for years, and eventually De Vaca and three others reached Mexico City. He wrote his memoirs, but because he had little knowledge of exactly where he was, the book is unreliable in some ways; it does, however, present the first look at the Native Americans. His journey inspired expeditions by Hernando de Soto and Francisco Coronado. His book, *Relación*, remains in print five hundred years after he wrote it.

JONATHAN DICKINSON

Philadelphia

Jonathan Dickinson had no plans to come to Florida. He booked passage with his wife and infant son on the *Reformation* from Jamaica to Philadelphia. Their ship ran into problems, and three weeks later, they were blown ashore at what is now Hobe Sound. On shore, an Indian tribe stole their provisions and burned their ship. They saved a lifeboat and headed up the coast with the children and the sick in the boat, with the rest walking along the shore. They lost all their clothes to another Indian tribe and used pages from the Bible to cover themselves. They were rescued after nearly two months, but even with the accompaniment of Spanish soldiers, the journey to St. Augustine was difficult. Five passengers died of exposure. They reached Philadelphia on April 5, 1697, more than seven months after leaving Port Royal. Dickinson wrote a booklet about his experiences, and it became a bestseller on both sides of the Atlantic and gave the British their first view of Florida and the Indians. It was reprinted in Dutch and German. Dickinson was a Quaker,

Jonathan Dickinson endured an ordeal that produced a best-selling book.

and the Quakers promoted the book as a story of inspiration and pointed out that Dickinson had decided not to fight the Indians but followed the doctrine of pacifism and survived. *Jonathan Dickinson's Journal* remains in print after four hundred years.

ZANE GREY

Long Key

Author Zane Grey is best known for his books on the West, but he loved writing about Florida. He published his first bestseller in 1910, *The Heritage of the Desert*, and he came to Florida by accident a year later. He was on his way to Mexico when he learned of an outbreak of smallpox there and ended up at Long Key. That led to an article for the magazine *Field and Stream* and a return trip a year later. His bestseller *Riders of the Purple Sage* had just been published, and he became one of the best-known writers in the country. He became a regular in Florida and organized a fishing club whose membership included Franklin Roosevelt and Herbert Hoover. He wrote a book, *Tales of Southern Rivers*, which was far different from his other books. When his writing drew tourists to Long Key, he could no longer find the solitude he yearned for and moved to other fishing sites.

He usually stayed in a cottage at Henry Flagler's Long Key Fishing Camp. It is still there and available for rent. It is on the ocean, and the San Pedro Archaeological Preserve is nearby. (Check out keyshistory.org/longkey.html for more information about the camp.)

MARJORIE KINNAN RAWLINGS

Cross Creek

Marjorie Kinnan Rawlings moved to Cross Creek with her husband to find the solitude to write. Her husband preferred more excitement, and the marriage ended. Cross Creek is a small community south of Gainesville that Rawlings described as "a primitive section off the beaten path, where men hunted and fished and worked small groves and farms for a meager living." They purchased a small house, and she found inspiration all around her. In 1931, she sold an article to *Scribner's Magazine* called "Cracker Chidlings," which captured the flavor and accents of Cross Creek. The article drew the attention of F. Scott Fitzgerald, Thomas Wolfe and Ernest Hemingway. The nation's leading editor, Maxwell Perkins, was also impressed and became her editor. Her books were about the people who lived in Cross Creek. In 1938, she published her classic, *The Yearling*, which became a bestseller and a motion picture. Her neighbors were surprised to see their lives captured in the pages of her book and on the movie screen—a few were angered. In 1940, she married Norton Baskin, who owned a hotel in St. Augustine that Rawlings had invested in. She died in 1953.

Her home is located between Gainesville and Ocala on County Road 325. It is now a state park and remains much as it was when she lived there. It is possible to imagine that she just stepped out and will return in a few minutes. Her typewriter is waiting for her. The hotel Norton Baskin owned in St. Augustine was once the residence of William Warden, a partner in Standard Oil Company. Baskin purchased it in 1941 and turned it into a hotel. He and Rawlings had an apartment on the top floor. In 1950, it became Ripley's Believe It or Not! and has been a major tourist attraction since then.

F. SCOTT FITZGERALD

St. Petersburg Beach

F. Scott Fitzgerald and his wife, Zelda, were a perfect match in the 1920s. He chronicled the lives of the rich and those who sought to be rich. With the publication of *This Side of Paradise*, he became the chronicler of his generation. He and Zelda lived recklessly—she suffered from mental problems and he was an alcoholic. He frequented Florida, visiting friends in the new center of wealth, Palm Beach, but preferring the Don Cesar Hotel in St. Petersburg Beach. The sprawling pink hotel opened in 1928 just as the Florida land boom was crashing. Fitzgerald foresaw the problems the hotel would face. "The hotel was almost empty and there were so many waiters waiting to be off that we could hardly eat our meals." At the Don Cesar, he completed writing *Tender Is the Night*, but he also suffered tragedy there. In 1932, Zelda suffered a breakdown at the hotel and was taken

The Don Cesar was built during the land boom of the 1920s and played host to gangster Al Capone, presidents and celebrities. It was a favorite of writer F. Scott Fitzgerald and his wife, Zelda. He wrote *Tender Is the Night* at the hotel.

to a clinic in Baltimore. He set two of his short stories in Florida. "The Rich Boy" deals with one of Fitzgerald's favorite themes, the gap between rich and poor. The lead character was modeled after his close friend and Princeton classmate Ludlow Fowler. He also wrote "The Offshore Pirate," which was published in the *Saturday Evening Post*. The story is about a group of phony pirates who kidnap a wealthy woman onboard her yacht off the Florida coast. The young woman and one of the pirates fall in love, and there is a happy ending.

When he was in Palm Beach, Fitzgerald stayed at The Breakers, which has the same grandeur it had nearly a century ago.

FRANK SLAUGHTER

Jacksonville

Frank Slaughter was working as a doctor in Jacksonville when he purchased a sixty-dollar typewriter and launched his writing career. He wrote story after story, but his rejection slips piled up. He sold one article in five years—for twelve dollars, far less than he had paid for the typewriter. His break came when Marjorie Kinnan Rawlings was admitted to the hospital, and he saw a chance to get a patron. She agreed to read fifteen pages of his work, but she advised him to "stick to operating." In a way, that was what he did. He wrote a book about medicine with a political angle, *That None Should Die.* It was rejected by publisher after publisher until a local librarian helped him obtain a publisher. After several rewrites, it became a bestseller. He went on to write forty novels that became bestsellers. The publishers were amazed by his eye for detail and his plots, but his writing was still terrible. That was easily solved by hiring ghost writers to take his plots and turn them into literary works. Several of his books became movies, including *Sangaree, Doctor's Wives, The Story of Ruth* and *Naked in the Sun.*

THEODORE PRATT

Lake Worth

Theodore Pratt may be one of the least-known best-selling writers in the United States. He came to Florida in 1934 and settled in Lake Worth, where he wrote thirty-five novels, including fourteen set in Florida. They are marked by both detailed historical research and wild flights of fancy. The detailed research is shown in his book *The Barefoot Mailman*, which tells the story of the first man to deliver mail in South Florida. He had to walk along the beach because there were no roads. It was made into a movie starring Robert Cummings. An example of his flights of fantasy is his book *The Incredible Mr. Limpet*, a 1942 book about a mild-mannered bookkeeper who turns into a fish that helps the navy spot German submarines. It was made into a movie starring Don Knotts. He did extensive research for his book *Mercy Island*, including spending time in the Florida Keys to learn

Author Thomas Pratt is largely forgotten today, but he wrote a series of bestsellers, including *The Barefoot Mailman* and "Land of the Jook," both of which were made into movies.

about fishing and sailing. It was made into a movie with Ray Middleton and Gloria Dickson. His article "Land of the Jook" caused a national stir for exposing the squalid working conditions among migrant workers in South Florida. He wrote, "Many of the migrants, white and black, continue to live in indescribable squalor in ramshackle camps, boardinghouses, tin and burlap shacks, broken down trailers, trucks, old automobiles." It became a movie with Ronald Reagan and Ann Sheridan. When Pratt died in 1969, he turned his papers over to the relatively new Florida Atlantic University. They can be seen in the Pratt Room of FAU's Wimberly Library. His old desk is there, along with his office chair.

WALT WHITMAN
New York

Walt Whitman owned a drawing of the great Florida Indian Chief Osceola, which inspired Whitman to write the poem "Osceola" in tribute to the chief's death in the custody of American soldiers. Whitman said that as a young man he had met a marine who told him the story of the death of Osceola. The army offered Osceola a truce to negotiate peace during the Seminole Indian War, but when he agreed to negotiate, he was captured and imprisoned. He died in captivity, and the attending physician cut off his head for a souvenir. Using the description provided by the soldier, Whitman wrote:

> *When his hour for death had come,*
> *He slowly raised himself from the bed on the floor,*
> *Drew on his war-dress, shirt, leggings, and girdled the belt around his waist…*

Whitman never came to Florida, but he dreamed about it constantly. In 1888, the Northeast endured one of the worst blizzards in history. Over a four-day period, nearly a dozen inches of snow fell, trapping Whitman in his New Jersey home. It inspired him to write "Orange Buds by Mail from Florida" about receiving some orange buds from Florida. He wrote the poem for the *New York Herald*, and newspapers throughout the blizzard-hit region reprinted it.

Chief Osecola was captured by trickery under a flag of truce and died while in army custody. Even though he had attacked American troops, the method of his capture generated great sympathy.

HENRY JAMES

Palm Beach

By 1904, Henry James had published a string of successful novels, including *Daisy Miller* and *Washington Square*. For his next project, he planned to tour the United States and write a series of essays about the different regions. It was designed to be a travelogue but instead became a commentary on Americans. He was shocked at what he saw as the American rush to materialism. The last chapter of *The American Scene* was so controversial that his American publisher cut it from the book. His travels brought him to Palm Beach, a barren scrub just a few years earlier that Henry Flagler was transforming into a playground for the wealthy. His essay on Palm Beach described the shops "dealing, naturally, in commodities almost beyond price."

JACK KEROUAC

Orlando

Jack Kerouac came to Orlando in 1956, unknown as he stepped from the New York bus onto a downtown street. Within a year, he became one of the most famous writers in the nation and the king of the beat writers. His mother wanted him in Orlando to unite what was a fractured family. He stayed only a few weeks but returned the next year and moved to a small wooden house in the city's College Park neighborhood. He had written his classic *On the Road* in 1951 but could not find a publisher. Two months after he moved to Orlando, his book was published to great acclaim. As his fame grew, he remained in Orlando writing his second book, *The Dharma Bums*. But that did not have nearly the same success as *On the Road*. He bought land in the Orlando suburbs and dreamed of building a house for his mother, sister, brother-in-law and himself. But like much of his life, it was only a dream and nothing came of it. He later moved to St. Petersburg, where he drank heavily and tried with little success to write. In 1969, he died in St. Petersburg. He was forty-seven years old, but a nurse attending him said, "I thought he was much older."

The Kerouac home in Orlando is at 1418 Clouser Avenue. It is used for author events and offers a residency program for emerging writers (details at kerouacproject.org).

HARRY CREWS

Gainesville

When Harry Crews died in 2012, the *New York Times* wrote, "Crews was renowned for darkly comic, bitingly satirical, grotesquely populated and almost preternaturally violent novels." He avoided the bestseller list, but by the time he died at the age of seventy-six, he had developed a loyal following. His childhood was a series of horrors. He wrote that his family was so poor "there was not enough cash money in the county to close up a dead man's eyes," and people ate clay. He escaped to the marines and served in the Korean War. He used his GI Bill benefits to attend the University of Florida and taught at a community college before being hired to teach at the University of Florida. In 1968, he published his first novel, *The Gospel Singer*; his books featured a sociopath, a sideshow freak and even a character who ate a 1971 Fort Maverick. He was once asked why his books were not more upbeat, and he said, "Listen, if you want to write about all sweetness and light and that stuff, go get a job at Hallmark."

60 BOOKS

RAYMOND ARSENAULT,
ST. PETERSBURG AND THE FLORIDA DREAM, 1888–1950
(University Press of Florida)

One of Florida's best historians tells the story of St. Petersburg, a city founded by a Russian immigrant and named for his hometown. It is told well and is more than a "Florida Dream"—it is the story of millions of Americans who have dreamed of retiring to paradise.

WILLIAM BARTRAM,
THE TRAVELS OF WILLIAM BARTRAM
(Dover)

Naturalist William Bartram first came to Florida in 1766 to build a plantation near present-day Jacksonville. The plantation failed, and he left the state but returned several years later to collect natural history specimens throughout the South. He arrived in Florida the following year. The result

William Bartram traveled throughout the South, collecting natural history specimens. His book gave the world the first in-depth look at Florida.

of his journey was one of the first bestsellers in the New World and an in-depth look at Florida. Its fame spread to Europe, where it inspired other writers, including poets William Wordsworth and Samuel Taylor Coleridge. The book remains in print more than two centuries after it was published.

SUSAN BRADEN,
ARCHITECTURE OF LEISURE: THE FLORIDA RESORT HOTELS OF HENRY FLAGLER AND HENRY PLANT
(University Press of Florida)

Architectural historian Susan Braden traces the development of the grand resort hotel beginning in the 1850s. The rise of the hotels mirrored the rise of great wealth in the United States and improvement in transportation brought on by the coming of the railroad. The two Henrys, Plant and Flagler, were the master builders of resorts in Florida and created the tourist industry that came to dominate the state's economy. The two were railroad builders but realized that to sell tickets they would need something to draw customers. The result was some of the grand hotels; two of the finest, the Tampa Bay Hotel and the Ponce de Leon, still stand.

SETH BRAMSON,
L'CHAIM!: THE HISTORY OF THE JEWISH COMMUNITY OF GREATER MIAMI
(The History Press)

Isidor Cohen came to Miami in 1896, the same year the city was born. He was the first of hundreds of thousands of Jewish residents to call Miami home. Bramson traces the history and impact of those who came to make the city what it has become today.

LOREN G. BROWN,
TOTCH: A LIFE IN THE EVERGLADES
(University Press of Florida)

Few men have lived as Totch Brown did, and few men knew the Everglades quite as well. The book is at once a history of a bygone era, a memoir and a confession. Brown began as an alligator hunter and fisherman, barely surviving before turning to smuggling marijuana and the big money it brought. The big money took him to prison on tax evasion. It is also the story of the twentieth century in the Everglades with the growth and problems that became apparent.

RACHEL CARSON,
THE SEA AROUND US
(Oxford University Press)

A decade before the publication of her classic *Silent Spring*, author Rachel Carson focused on the problems of the sea, particularly in Florida. *The Sea Around Us* became a bestseller and was one of the first books to sound the alarm on the coming ecological damage. She spent much time in the Florida Keys to gather material, explored the Everglades and went diving off the Florida coast.

JAMES C. CLARK,
A CONCISE HISTORY OF FLORIDA
(The History Press)

An overview of Florida history presented in an easy-to-read manner. The volume covers everything from the first native settlers to the twenty-first century.

JAMES C. CLARK,
PRESIDENTS IN FLORIDA: HOW THE PRESIDENTS HAVE SHAPED FLORIDA AND HOW FLORIDA HAS INFLUENCED THE PRESIDENTS
(Pineapple Press)

From George Washington to Donald Trump, whether it was politics or international issues, Florida has played a leading role in national events and in every presidency.

JAMES C. CLARK,
200 QUICK LOOKS AT FLORIDA HISTORY
(Pineapple Press)

This collection of newspaper columns from the *Orlando Sentinel* tells two hundred brief stories about Florida history. They offer a quick overview of the leading people and events that shaped Florida.

DAVID R. COLBURN,
RACIAL CHANGE AND COMMUNITY CRISIS
(University Press of Florida)

Florida's role in the civil rights movement seldom draws the attention given to other southern states, but the violence in Florida was significant. The worst was in St. Augustine, where civil rights marchers led by Dr. Martin Luther King Jr. found vicious opposition. Colburn, one of the leading Florida historians, tells the story of the conflict and the outcome in the oldest city in the United States.

DAVID R. COLBURN AND JANE LANDERS,
THE AFRICAN AMERICAN HERITAGE OF FLORIDA
(University Press of Florida)

Few realize the role African Americans played in the founding of Florida. There were Africans with the earliest Spanish expeditions to explore Florida, and the community known as Fort Mose was the earliest free black settlement in the New World. African Americans fought in all three Seminole wars, but their story had gone untold until Colburn and Landers brought it to light.

DONALD WALTER CURL,
THE BOCA RATON RESORT AND CLUB: MIZNER'S INN
(The History Press)

Addison Mizner found success and wealth in building homes and other buildings in Palm Beach. It was Mizner who gave the town the look it has today. Like many Florida developers in the 1920s, he had big dreams, and Mizner's was to build a resort community at Boca Raton. To start, he built the Cloister Inn, which was designed to house the wealthy who were potential buyers in his development. A hurricane in 1926 not only caused widespread destruction but also killed the Florida land boom and Mizner's dream. The buyers disappeared, but the Cloisters remained. The name was changed to the Boca Raton Resort & Club, and it became one of the grandest luxury resorts on the Florida coast. Curl tells the rich story of the resort and the community it started.

JACK E. DAVIS,
AN EVERGLADES PROVIDENCE: MARJORY STONEMAN DOUGLAS AND THE AMERICAN ENVIRONMENTAL CENTURY
(University of Georgia Press)

Marjory Stoneman Douglas was a champion of the environmental movement in Florida, the first voice raised to preserve the Everglades beginning in the 1940s and continuing into the twenty-first century.

JACK E. DAVIS,
THE GULF: THE MAKING OF AN AMERICAN SEA
(Liveright Publishing)

Jack Davis, a professor at the University of Florida, has emerged as one of the nation's leading environmental historians. His Pulitzer Prize–winning book gives the Gulf of Mexico its place in history. His book is beautifully written and establishes the Gulf as "America's Sea."

KATHLEEN A. DEAGAN AND DARCIE A. MACMAHON,
FORT MOSE: COLONIAL AMERICA'S BLACK FORTRESS OF FREEDOM
(University Press of Florida)

Fort Mose was the first free African American settlement in the New World, established by the Spanish as a refuge for slaves escaping from the Carolinas and Georgia. It survived until the English invaded, but its story is one of the most dramatic and long overlooked in Florida history.

ALEJANDRO M. DE QUESADA,
A HISTORY OF FLORIDA FORTS: FLORIDA'S LONELY OUTPOSTS
(The History Press)

If there is one thing Florida has had plenty of, it is forts. Five nations have built forts in Florida over more than four centuries. The French and the Spanish came first, then the British, the Americans and finally the Confederates. There are still several forts standing, along with re-creations of forts and cities that remind us they began as forts—Fort Lauderdale and Fort Myers. This is the ultimate guide to the forts that shaped Florida.

JOAN DIDION,
MIAMI
(Vintage)

Famed writer Joan Didion uses her literary skills to capture the essence of Miami in the last half of the twentieth century. Her focus is on the Cuban community, beginning with Fidel Castro's attempts to raise money in the city to overthrow the Batista regime and leading to the Cuban refugees making endless plans to overthrow Castro.

MARJORY STONEMAN DOUGLAS,
THE EVERGLADES: RIVER OF GRASS
(Pineapple Press)

The book and the lifelong campaign by its author turned the Everglades from what was considered a worthless swamp into what is now viewed as a valuable resource, giving life to South Florida. The book came out as the federal government was making the Everglades a national park, which seemed like a blessing, but this has not stopped the threats to the Everglades.

MARTIN A. DYCKMAN,
FLORIDIAN OF HIS CENTURY: THE COURAGE OF GOVERNOR LEROY COLLINS
(University Press of Florida)

In 1968, the voters of Florida rejected Leroy Collins when he ran for the United States Senate. It ended his political career, but today he is viewed as the greatest governor in Florida's history. He led the state through one of its most tumultuous periods, the early days of the civil rights movement, which saw violence in many southern states. Dyckman's book is excellent in discussing Collins and the 1950s in Florida.

RICHARD FOGLESONG,
MARRIED TO THE MOUSE: WALT DISNEY WORLD AND ORLANDO
(Yale University Press)

The coming of Walt Disney World to Orlando changed the city and the state. Foglesong, a professor at Rollins College, tells the story, which has more twists and turns than a mystery novel. Disney secretly bought tens of thousands of acres using second, third and fourth parties as fronts to keep the deals secret and keep the prices down. Then there was the drama of obtaining zoning changes and passing legislation to give Disney sweeping powers. Foglesong tells the story well.

MICHAEL GANNON,
OPERATION DRUMBEAT: THE DRAMATIC TRUE STORY OF GERMANY'S FIRST U-BOAT ATTACKS ALONG THE AMERICAN COAST IN WORLD WAR II
(Harper Perennial)

Michael Gannon was one of the greatest historians in Florida history. While researching a book on another topic, he came across the story of German submarine action along the Florida coast at the beginning of World War II. His book became a bestseller and the definitive volume on the Nazi drama taking place just miles from the Florida coast.

PAUL GEORGE,
LITTLE HAVANA
(Arcadia Publishing)

The city within a city has become home to those who came to Cuba after Castro came to power. George, the preeminent Miami historian, tells the story of Little Havana's rise and its place in the history of Florida and the nation.

THOMAS GRAHAM,
MR. FLAGLER'S ST. AUGUSTINE
(University Press of Florida)

When Henry Flagler found St. Augustine, it was a poor fishing village, a remnant of the past with little to look forward to. Soon it was the winter playground of the wealthy and the first stop on Flagler's empire that ended in Key West.

GUILLERMO J. GRENIER AND CORINNA J. MOEBIUS,
A HISTORY OF LITTLE HAVANA
(The History Press)

When Fidel Castro came to power in 1959, he set off a mass exodus to Florida. There were some short-lived attempts to disperse the refugees throughout the nation, but in the end, the vast majority of Cubans settled in Miami. The center of their new lives became known as Little Havana. Grenier and Moebius trace the history from farmland to vibrant city within a city.

PATRICIA C. GRIFFIN,
MULLET ON THE BEACH:
THE MINORCANS OF FLORIDA, 1768–1788
(University Press of Florida)

The Minorcans endured enormous pain as they sought a home in Florida. Griffin's book describes the first twenty years of their ordeal. The Minorcans came to British East Florida in 1768 to work on an indigo plantation. They endured unspeakable horrors before revolting and escaping to St. Augustine, where they became a key part of the growing community.

MICHAEL GRUNWALD,
THE SWAMP: THE EVERGLADES, FLORIDA, AND POLITICS OF PARADISE
(Simon & Schuster)

It is amazing to think that a succession of Florida governors spent their administrations trying to drain or pave the Everglades. Grunwald captures the rich history from the ice age to the twenty-first century. Today, most people realize the threat to the Everglades, but it is still fighting for its life.

JULIANNE HARE,
TALLAHASSEE: A CAPITAL CITY HISTORY
(Arcadia Publishing)

There were once two Floridas, East and West, and each had its own capital, in St. Augustine and Pensacola. When Florida was acquired by the United States, there was a plan to keep both capitals and alternate legislative sessions. It didn't work, and a spot halfway between the two towns became the capital: Tallahassee. Hare traces the history from earliest settlement to the city's place as the capital of the nation's third-largest state.

RACKHAM HOLT,
MARY McLEOD BETHUNE: A BIOGRAPHY
(Doubleday & Company)

Starting with just five dollars and supplies salvaged from a nearby scrapyard, Mary Bethune launched what has become Bethune-Cookman University. She made friends with the powerful, from Franklin Roosevelt to John D. Rockefeller, and became a national figure.

ZORA NEALE HURSTON,
THEIR EYES WERE WATCHING GOD
(Harper Perennial)

This is Hurston's most important novel. Originally published in 1937, it created a stir when it came out but then faded along with Hurston's career. Because of the efforts of Alice Walker and others, Hurston and her book were rescued from obscurity. She wrote it in just seven weeks while on a Guggenheim Fellowship in Haiti. Like Hurston, the main character settles in Eatonville, an all-black community outside Orlando.

GLORIA JAHODA,
THE OTHER FLORIDA
(Florida Classics Library)

For the tens of millions of tourists who come to Florida each year, Orlando and its theme parks are the center of the world. Nearly half a century ago, Gloria Jahoda moved to Tallahassee and saw that people were missing a great deal. Her book is about moonshiners, small-town preachers and the residents of the back roads. But the key to the book is her appreciation of the Florida landscape and wildlife.

JAMES WELDON JOHNSON,
THE AUTOBIOGRAPHY OF AN EX-COLORED MAN
(Hill and Wang)

James Weldon Johnson grew up in Jacksonville, became principal of an all–African American school and then went to New York, where he became head of the National Association for the Advancement of Colored People. His novel is the story of a biracial man in the late 1800s and early 1900s.

GILBERT KING,
DEVIL IN THE GROVE: THURGOOD MARSHALL, THE GROVELAND BOYS, AND THE DAWN OF A NEW AMERICA
(Harper Perennial)

King won a Pulitzer Prize for his book on the Groveland Four and almost certainly a pardon for the eponymous four for the injustice carried out against them by a brutal sheriff and a repressive legal system. The case involved future Supreme Court justice Thurgood Marshall, who defended two of the four.

JOHN D. MACDONALD,
CONDOMINIUM: A NOVEL
(Random House Trade Paperbacks)

When writer John D. MacDonald came to Sarasota, it was a small community. Thanks to his fame and friends, he helped build a substantial writers' colony that exists today. *Condominium* is a novel, but it is also an early warning (1977) about the dangers of overdevelopment on Florida's coast.

JOHN K. MAHON,
HISTORY OF THE SECOND SEMINOLE WAR, 1835–1842
(University Press of Florida)

The three Florida wars with the Seminole Indians are almost forgotten today, despite their intensity and cost. The Second Seminole War was the longest and most expensive. The result of the war was the removal of most of the Seminole Indians from Florida. The remaining Seminoles fled to the Everglades.

WALTER MARTIN, FLORIDA'S FLAGLER
(University of Georgia)

This was the first full-length biography of Henry Flagler and covers his entire life, from his poverty-stricken childhood to becoming one of the nation's wealthiest men, responsible for drawing the first tourists to Florida in large numbers.

SUSAN CAROL McCARTHY, LAY THAT TRUMPET IN OUR HANDS
(Bantam Books)

Officially, this is a novel, the story of a twelve-year-old girl in an era when the Ku Klux Klan spread terror throughout Central Florida. In fact, Susan Carol McCarthy is telling the true story of the violence in the state and her father's efforts to help the Federal Bureau of Investigation stop it.

STUART B. McIVER, DEATH IN THE EVERGLADES: THE MURDER OF GUY BRADLEY, AMERICA'S FIRST MARTYR TO ENVIRONMENTALISM
(University Press of Florida)

Guy Bradley was one of the nation's first game wardens. His job was to protect the wading birds from hunters. It seems hard to imagine today, but feathers from the birds were literally worth their weight in gold. They were used as decorations on women's hats around the turn of the twentieth century. When he tried to enforce the ban on bird hunting, he was shot and killed when he stopped a man and his two sons hunting egrets in the Everglades.

Guy Bradley died trying to protect Florida's rare birds as the state's first environmentalist.

JOHN A. McPHEE,
ORANGES
(Farrar, Straus and Giroux)

This book began as an article in *The New Yorker* magazine. More than anything ever written about the state's top cash crop, the book captures the people of the industry and the problems they face. It is well written.

JERALD MILANICH,
FLORIDA INDIANS AND THE INVASION FROM EUROPE
(University Press of Florida)

When people think of Indians in Florida, they almost always think of the Seminoles. The Seminoles were relatively late in coming, and there were many tribes that came before them. Most were wiped out by the diseases the Spanish brought with them, as Milanich tells us. This is a solid retelling of a lost chapter in Florida history.

GARY MONROE,
THE HIGHWAYMEN: FLORIDA'S AFRICAN AMERICAN LANDSCAPE PAINTERS
(University Press of Florida)

The story of the African American painters known as "the Highwaymen" is one of the most remarkable in the art world. A.E. Backus, a painter who built his reputation on landscape paintings, took a group of African American youngsters under his wing and taught them to paint. They began by selling their paintings along the highways for a few dollars, but gradually their work was noticed and today sells for hundreds and thousands of dollars.

GARY ROSS MORMINO,
LAND OF SUNSHINE, STATE OF DREAMS:
A SOCIAL HISTORY OF MODERN FLORIDA
(University Press of Florida)

At the beginning of World War II, Florida was the least-populated state in the nation. As hundreds of thousands of soldiers flooded into the state to train, that began to change. Within a few years, Florida was the fastest-growing state in the nation. Mormino, one of Florida's leading historians, traces the explosive growth of the state.

JOHN MUIR,
A THOUSAND-MILE WALK TO THE GULF
(Dover Publications)

In 1876, John Muir began walking from Indiana, crossed Tennessee, the Carolinas and Georgia and then finally came to Florida. Here Muir chronicles the wilderness he found and the people he met along the way. It is the best look at Florida in the late 1800s.

STEVEN NOLL AND DAVID TEGEDER,
DITCH OF DREAMS: THE CROSS FLORIDA BARGE
CANAL AND THE STRUGGLE FOR FLORIDA'S FUTURE
(University Press of Florida)

A cross-Florida barge canal may have been Florida's longest-running dream. The early Spanish first thought of building a water route across the state, and it took four centuries for the dream to finally die. Noll and Tegeder expertly weave the story of how close it came to reality and what it would have done to the state's environment.

CRAIG PITTMAN,
OH, FLORIDA!: HOW AMERICAS WEIRDEST STATE INFLUENCES THE REST OF THE COUNTRY
(St. Martin's Press)

Using true stories, Pittman captures Florida as few writers have. A veteran reporter, he brings a journalist's eye to the kinds of things that only seem to happen in Florida.

CRAIG PITTMAN,
THE SCENT OF SCANDAL: GREED, BETRAYAL, AND THE WORLD'S MOST BEAUTIFUL ORCHID
(University Press of Florida)

The subject is orchids, but Pittman weaves an unrivaled mystery based on the theft of one of the world's most valuable orchids. The characters would stop at nothing to possess the orchid.

THEODORE PRATT,
THE BAREFOOT MAILMAN
(Florida Classics Library)

Florida really did have a barefoot mailman at one time. Before South Florida had roads, the mail was easier to deliver by following the coastline. The book is fiction but based on fact and portrays life as it was in early Florida.

MARJORIE KINNAN RAWLINGS,
THE YEARLING
(Aladdin Classics)

Rawlings came to Florida to find tranquility for her writing. What she found were characters to use in her greatest works. *The Yearling*, which became a Pulitzer Prize winner and a major motion picture, features the people and events Rawlings found in rural Florida.

ROBERT REDD,
ST. AUGUSTINE AND THE CIVIL WAR
(The History Press)

St. Augustine has been held by four nations and attacked by an equal number since 1565. The massive fort there was seized by the Confederates at the start of the Civil War and then retaken by the United States. Historian Robert Redd's well-researched and well-written history tells the story of the small town with the big fort.

DIANE ROBERTS,
DREAM STATE: EIGHT GENERATIONS OF SWAMP LAWYERS, CONQUISTADORS, CONFEDERATE DAUGHTERS, BANANA REPUBLICS, AND OTHER FLORIDA WILDLIFE
(Free Press)

Every few years, an author writes a book that captures Florida in a single volume. Diane Roberts draws on her family experiences in the state and throws in commentary on the way things have turned out. Her family first came to Florida in time to fight Indians and help build the state. She takes her story up to the controversial 2000 presidential election.

JERRELL H. SHOFNER,
NOR IS IT OVER YET: FLORIDA IN THE ERA OF RECONSTRUCTION, 1863–1877
(University Press of Florida)

Shofner's book is the classic work on Reconstruction in Florida. Like all southern states, Florida went through Reconstruction, but its experience was far different. There had been few battles in the state, so there was not the widespread damage as in other states. But the people of the state were left destitute, and the limited mileage of rails in the state suffered significant damage.

LILLIAN E. SMITH,
THE KILLERS OF THE DREAM
(Norton)

Smith spent her life fighting injustice in the South. Her book is a memoir, starting with her childhood and tracing the discrimination she found everywhere she looked. The book was published in 1949 and was one of the first indictments of the Jim Crow South. It had vast influence, coming at the start of the modern civil rights movement.

PATRICK D. SMITH,
A LAND REMEMBERED
(Pineapple Press)

If Florida had a state book, it would be *A Land Remembered*. The novel traces three generations of the MacIveys, who came to frontier Florida and endured hardship and poverty before advancing to wealthy developers. The book is beautifully written.

IRVIN D. SOLOMON,
THOMAS EDISON: THE FORT MYERS CONNECTION
(Arcadia Publishing)

Fort Myers, a one-time army base, was little more than a village in Southwest Florida when Thomas Edison discovered it in 1885. For nearly a half century, it was his home away from home. He convinced his friend Henry Ford to become a part-time resident, and the two drew notables from Harvey Firestone to writer John Burroughs. Solomon tells a little-known story about Edison and his long-lasting impact on Fort Myers.

LES STANDIFORD, LAST TRAIN TO PARADISE: HENRY FLAGLER AND THE SPECTACULAR RISE AND FALL OF THE RAILROAD THAT CROSSED AN OCEAN
(Thorndike Press)

Novelist Lee Standiford took on the subject of one of the greatest engineering challenges of the twentieth century and wrote a beautiful book about it. The nonfiction book tells the story of Henry Flagler and the successful completion of his final dream.

DANA STE. CLAIRE, CRACKER: THE CRACKER CULTURE IN FLORIDA HISTORY
(University Press of Florida)

Floridians can't agree if calling someone a "cracker" is a positive or a negative. The term goes back some two hundred years, and most agree that the term comes from the noise a whip made as a Florida cattleman drove his herd. Some see a cracker as a Florida pioneer who helped open Florida through hard work. Others see it as a slur or derogative term for whites.

HARRIET BEECHER STOWE, PALMETTO LEAVES
(Echo Library)

There is great irony in that Harriet Beecher Stowe's writing both hurt and helped Florida. Her first book, *Uncle Tom's Cabin*, stirred passions in both the North and the South and played a role in starting the Civil War. After the war, she came to Florida, purchased a plantation and wrote a book that promoted tourism in Florida. The book is an early plug for the wonders of the state, and it served as a drawing card for people who took her advice.

ROBERT A. TAYLOR,
REBEL STOREHOUSE: FLORIDA IN THE CONFEDERATE ECONOMY
(University of Alabama Press)

Florida sent the fewest number of men to fight for the Confederacy and saw just two battles. Nevertheless, Florida played a key role as a supply depot to the Confederates. Because Florida saw little combat, its cattle and crops could be raised without the worry of military occupation. As Taylor found, Florida's contribution turns out to have been vital.

JULES VERNE,
FROM THE EARTH TO THE MOON
(Dover Publications)

Jules Verne had an amazing imagination, as his many books show. *From the Earth to the Moon* is fiction, but it's still an amazingly accurate prediction of what would come a century later. Writing from France, Verne predicted a mission to the moon, but of the entire world, he chose Florida as the launch site. There are other touches that make this novel uncanny.

THOMAS WOLFE,
THE RIGHT STUFF
(Bantam Books)

The original seven Mercury astronauts seized the attention of the nation when they were first named. They had been obscure pilots from the navy, marines and air force when they were introduced to the nation. The book by Tom Wolfe captures those early days of the space program in Florida and how it changed the state and the world.

THE WPA GUIDE TO FLORIDA: THE FEDERAL WRITERS' PROJECT GUIDE TO 1930S FLORIDA
(Pantheon Books)

The Works Progress Administration was a creation of the Franklin Roosevelt administration to employ people during the Great Depression. Millions of people were employed in hundreds of fields. The WPA Guides to America consisted of guides to each of the states written by the unemployed writers who made up the Federal Writers' Project. The *Guide to Florida* came out near the end of the Great Depression and included contributions by the great African American writer Zora Neale Hurston. Coming out in 1939, the book captures the Florida that would soon disappear as the population exploded beginning in World War II.

10 ARCHIVES

P.K. YONGE LIBRARY OF FLORIDA HISTORY

Gainesville

This began as a private collection by P.K. Yonge and his son, Julien Yonge, in 1892. In 1945, the collection went to the University of Florida, where it formed the state's largest archive. Today, there are thirty-three thousand books and periodicals, 2,500 historic maps and thousands of photographs, postcards, manuscripts and other records. The collection is amazing, with letters by Marjorie Kinnan Rawlings, Senator David Levy Yulee and other key figures in state history. Many of the holdings are available online, ranging from Florida maps to diaries from the 1800s.

Alachua County, Map 2; http://guides.uflib.ufl.edu; 208 Smathers Library, Gainesville, Florida, 32611; 352-273-2778.

FLORIDA HISTORICAL SOCIETY

Cocoa

This is the state's oldest archives. Founded in 1856, it publishes the widely respected *Florida Historical Quarterly.* One of the collection's first items was *La Florida del Inca*, donated by Henry Flagler. The early collection was housed in the Cordova Hotel in St. Augustine. Today, it is in Historic Cocoa Village in the 1939 post office. There are more than eight thousand bound library volumes, including rare books, as well as ten thousand print photographs and fifteen thousand postcards.

Brevard County, Map 5; myfloridahistory.org; 435 Brevard Avenue, Cocoa, Florida, 32922; 321-690-1971.

FLORIDA STATE ARCHIVES
Tallahassee

It took 120 years, but in 1967, Florida finally created an archive in Tallahassee. Much of the state's history had already been lost, but the state has tried to make up for lost time. The collection includes legislative records dating back to 1821, as well as manuscripts of public officials and ordinary citizens. The photographic history is something special, with maps and more than 700,000 images of Florida from the early days of the camera. The collection also includes more than five thousand volumes of genealogical resources. There are also hundreds of videos dating from 1916 and covering politics, commerce and sports.

Leon County, Map 3; floridamemory.com; 500 South Bronough Street, Tallahassee, Florida, 32399; 850-245-6600.

THE STATE LIBRARY OF FLORIDA
Tallahassee

When Florida became a state, the first legislature authorized a library to collect official state records, maps and books. But it took eighty years before provisions were made for a state library. For those doing research into Florida and its history, it is an invaluable resource. The historic map collection of cities is excellent, and the documents include original Spanish land grants. It houses a large collection of city directories dating from the early twentieth century and campaign literature covering much of the twentieth century. A major feature of the library is the newspaper collection, which includes some five hundred different newspapers. It is a must stop for serious researchers. Like the State Archives, the State Library of Florida also has a number of videos.

Leon County, Map 3; dos.myflorida.com/library-archives; 500 South Bronough Street, Tallahassee, Florida, 32399; 850-245-6735.

FLORIDA STATE UNIVERSITY LIBRARY

Tallahassee

This collection contains editions of some of the first books about Florida, including William Bartram's *Travels through North and South Carolina, Georgia, East and West Florida* and a 1744 book about St. Augustine. There are extensive records of both the Spanish period and the British period. The library has significant records related to the Civil War. There are some records dealing with slavery, including a slave bill of sale from Jackson County. Some of the more interesting items are the records of stores that show the goods they carried and the prices paid. There is currency from different periods of Florida history, including Confederate money, and thousands of documents related to movies shown in Florida, including movie trailers from the Florida Theater in Tallahassee.

Leon County, Map 3; lib.fsu.edu; 116 Honors Way, Tallahassee, Florida, 32306; 850-644-2706.

WEST FLORIDA HISTORY CENTER
Pensacola

The University of West Florida specializes in the history of Pensacola and the Panhandle. West Florida has one of the strangest histories, containing parts of Louisiana, Alabama, Georgia and Mississippi over the centuries. The University of West Florida houses papers of major companies, including leading lumber companies and railroads, and information about the significant families from the early days of West Florida.

Escambia County, Map 3; libguides.uwf.edu/universityarchives; 11000 University Parkway, Pensacola, Florida, 32514; 850-474-2000.

ST. AUGUSTINE HISTORICAL SOCIETY
RESEARCH LIBRARY
St. Augustine

Organized in 1885, this site contains records relating to landownership in St. Augustine. There are also duplicates of records from the P.K. Yonge Library related to St. Augustine and St. Johns County. Included are photographs and books about the area.

St. Johns County, Map 2; saintaugustinehistoricalsociety.org; 271 Charlotte Street, St. Augustine, Florida, 32084; 904-824-2872.

UNIVERSITY OF SOUTH FLORIDA
SPECIAL COLLECTIONS
Tampa

These special collections have three main areas of concentration: the Tampa–St. Petersburg area, Cuba-Florida relations and African American studies. There are extensive records of former governor Leroy Collins, considered Florida's greatest governor. One of the more unusual aspects of the collection are the minutes of the Palm Beach Klavern of the Ku Klux Klan for 1927 and 1928.

Hillsborough County, Map 7; lib.usf.edu/special-collections; 4202 East Fowler Avenue, Tampa, Florida, 33620; 813-974-2731.

UNIVERSITY OF MIAMI SPECIAL COLLECTIONS
Miami

The library houses the papers of the environmentalist Marjory Stoneman Douglas and the Cuban Heritage Collection, which contains records from colonial times to the present. It has become the largest repository of Cuban-related documents outside of Cuba and Spain. One unusual part of the archives is the Cuban Theater Digital Archive, which includes extensive records of Cuban entertainment. Many of the records are now online for easy access.

Dade County, Map 6; library.miami.edu/specialcollections; 1300 Memorial Drive, Coral Gables, Florida, 33124; 305-284-3233.

THE MEEK-EATON BLACK ARCHIVES

Tallahassee

The Meek-Eaton archives are housed in the former main library at Florida A&M University. It was the first Carnegie library built on the campus of an African American land grant college. In 1971, the legislature called for a building to house material about African Americans, and the result is the Black Archives Research Center and Museum. The center is one of ten such archives in the United States and one of the largest, with nearly 500,000 documents and five thousand artifacts. The museum has a satellite location in downtown Tallahassee in the old Union Bank building, which was built by slaves in 1841.

Leon County, Map 3; famu.edu; 445 Gamble Street, Tallahassee, Florida, 32307; 850-599-3020.

The archives at Florida A&M University in Tallahassee house records related to African American history in Florida.

100 KEY DATES IN FLORIDA HISTORY

10,000 BC The first natives cross the land bridge from Siberia to Alaska and make their way to Florida during the ice age. They are called Paleo-Indians and come seeking food. They find mastodons, giant armadillos and horses. They also find a land mass that was twice as large as it is today.

9000 BC Glaciers begin to melt and sea levels rise, reducing Florida's land mass by about half.

5000 BC Archaeologists uncovered evidence that the natives had established settlements about this time. The Paleo-Indian culture gives way to the Archaic culture. The first settlements are usually on the coast.

AD 500 The Woodland culture emerges, marked by permanent settlements and relying on hunting deer and birds. The natives plant the first crops.

1200 The Mississippian culture emerges with a community structure led by chiefs, marked by widespread corn crops. There is evidence of trade throughout the peninsula.

1500 Spanish explorers sail through the Florida Straits as they seek wealth in the New World. In Florida, three large native groups dominate the peninsula: the Timucuas in Northeast and Central Florida, the Apalachees in the Big Bend area and the Calusas in South Florida. By 1550, more than 90 percent of the natives had died of diseases.

1513	Juan Ponce de León arrives and names the land "Pascua Florida" because his visit comes during the Feast of Flowers.
1521	Ponce de León returns to Florida, landing in South Florida to establish a colony. He is killed by natives.
1528	Spanish explorer Pánfilo de Narváez leads an ill-fated expedition into Florida with six hundred men. He dies, and just four of the original party survive and eventually arrive in Mexico City.
1539	Hernando de Soto lands with his eight-hundred-man expedition. They travel throughout the Southeast, and De Soto died on the banks of the Mississippi in 1542.
1559	Tristán de Luna y Arellano and his 1,500-man force attempt to settle present-day Pensacola (today the site of the Pensacola Naval Air Station), but the expedition fails; the remaining colonists return to Cuba within a year.
1562	Jean Ribault finds a site for a French Huguenot colony near present-day Jacksonville.
1564	French settlers under René de Laudonnière establish Fort Caroline near present-day Jacksonville.
1565	Pedro Menéndez de Avilés establishes St. Augustine, the first permanent European settlement in North America. He expels the French, and the Jesuits begin establishing missions throughout the Southeast.
1565	The Spanish attack Fort Caroline and kill most of the French.
1570	The first citrus groves are planted in St. Augustine.
1586	British seaman Sir Francis Drake attacks and burns St. Augustine.
1601	King Philip III of Spain commissions a map of Florida and says that he wants a fort built in Miami.
1603	The Spanish begin to build a mission chain across the peninsula.
1650	The missions extend to the Apalachicola River.
1672	Construction begins on Castillo de San Marcos, the sprawling fort to replace wooden structures that had been destroyed.
1698	After the first attempt fails, Pensacola is established by the Spanish.
1702	Over a two-year period, the English destroy many Spanish missions.
1715	A hurricane causes the sinking of the 1715 Spanish Treasure Fleet.

1719	The French briefly take control of Pensacola.
1738	Fort Mose, the first free black settlement in the New World, is established near St. Augustine.
1740	The English general James Oglethorpe invades St. Augustine but is unable to take the fort.
1743	The Spanish fail to establish a mission on Biscayne Bay.
1760	Natives from Georgia and Alabama move into Florida. Most are Creeks, but in Florida they are called Seminoles from the Spanish word *cimarron*, which means "outsiders" or "runaways."
1763	The French and Indian War (also known as the Seven Years' War) ends in victory for the British. During the war, Britain captures Cuba, and Spain offers to give them Florida in exchange for regaining Cuba. Britain will hold it until 1783. The British will divide Florida into East Florida and West Florida.

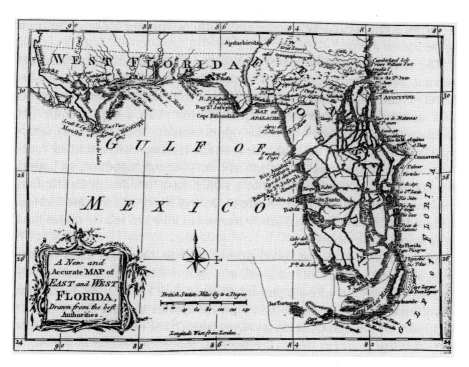

The British divided Florida into East and West Florida in 1763 but clearly had little idea of what they had acquired—they thought there was an extensive network of rivers in South Florida.

1768	The British begin cultivating sugar, citrus, rice and indigo.
1776	The American Revolution begins, but East and West Florida do not join the thirteen colonies. They become a refuge from Tories fleeing from the thirteen colonies.
1783	The final naval battle of the American Revolution is fought off Cape Canaveral.
1783	The American Revolution ends, and Britain gives Florida to Spain as part of the treaty.
1795	The United States and Spain sign the Treaty of San Lorenzo, establishing the 31st parallel as the northern boundary of Florida.
1816	Andrew Jackson invades Florida to fight the Seminole Indians. It is the start of the First Seminole War. The following year, there will be clashes between the American settlers, the Spanish, the remaining British agents and the Indians. Jackson burns native villages and captures St. Marks and Pensacola.
1819	Negotiations begin between Spain and the United States to acquire Florida. The result is the Adams-Onis Treaty in 1821.
1821	Florida becomes a United States territory, and Andrew Jackson briefly serves as its first governor.
1822	Florida Territory is formed from East Florida and part of West Florida.
1824	Tallahassee is established as the first permanent capital after attempts to divide the government between Pensacola and St. Augustine fail.
1824	Florida's first real lighthouse is established at St. Augustine.
1830	For the first time, Florida is included in the United States census and has a population of 34,730, including 18,395 whites and 16,335 nonwhites.
1832	Seminole and Miccosukee Indians sign the Treaty of Payne's Landing, under which the chiefs agree to move west of the Mississippi River. The treaty is controversial, and several chiefs say that they were forced into signing it.
1835	The Second Seminole War begins.
1842	The Second Seminole War ends, although there is no treaty and no conclusion.
1851	The legislature creates two colleges, West Florida Seminary and East Florida Seminary, which will become Florida State University and the University of Florida, respectively.

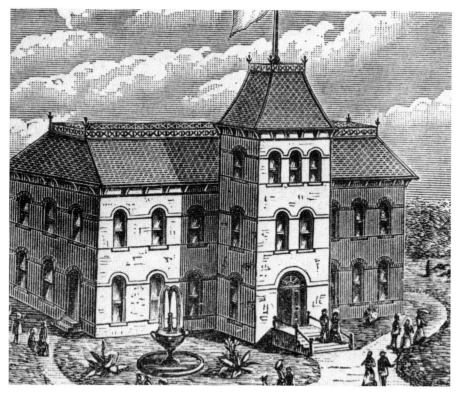

East Florida Seminary became the University of Florida.

1855	The Third Seminole War begins. It lasts until 1858.
1856	The Florida Historical Society is incorporated.
1861	A Secession Convention votes sixty-two to seven to leave the United States. On April 12, fighting begins at Fort Sumter, and in October, Confederate forces attack Fort Pickens on Santa Rosa Island in Pensacola.
1862	Union troops occupy St. Augustine and Jacksonville. Some fifteen thousand Florida men will serve in the Confederate army. The state's major contributions will be cattle, crops and salt.
1864	Confederate troops defeat Union soldiers at Olustee, the only major battle of the Civil War fought in Florida.
1865	The Civil War ends, and Florida governor John Milton commits suicide.

1876   Florida helps decide the controversial presidential election between Samuel Tilden and Rutherford B. Hayes. The election results are disputed, and eventually the electoral votes are awarded to Hayes, who ends Reconstruction in the South.

1878   Hullam Jones builds the first glass-bottom boat to attract tourists to Silver Springs.

1881   Philadelphia businessman Hamilton Disston purchases 4 million acres of land and fails in his attempt to drain it and build cities. He paid just twenty-five cents per acre for the land.

1887   Eatonville, Florida, is incorporated, the first African American town created after the Emancipation Proclamation. Florida A&M University opens as State Normal College for Colored Students.

1888   Florida begins shipping phosphate for use as fertilizer.

1891   Henry Plant opens the Tampa Bay Hotel—today part of the University of Tampa.

1894–95   A pair of devastating freezes nearly destroys the state's citrus crop.

Huge crowds turned out to see Henry Flagler's East Coast Railway off on its first trip to Key West.

Two freezes in the 1890s decimated the Florida orange industry. They forced the orange growers to move farther south.

1896	Henry Flagler's Florida East Coast Railway reaches Miami.
1898	The Spanish-American War sees thousands of soldiers establish camps in Tampa, Miami and Jacksonville.
1900	James Weldon Johnson and J. Rosamond Johnson write "Lift Every Voice and Sing," often considered the "Black national anthem."
1901	Fire burns down much of Jacksonville.
1904	Mary McLeod Bethune opens her school in Daytona Beach. It becomes Bethune-Cookman University.
1913	Henry Flagler's railroad reaches Key West.
1914	The nation's first scheduled airline flights begin between St. Petersburg and Tampa. The airline lasts just a few months.
1920	The Florida land boom begins.
1926	A massive hurricane strikes Florida, causing widespread damage and beginning the end of the Florida land boom.

In 1901, a fire destroyed most of downtown Jacksonville. It is the third-worst city fire in United States history behind the San Francisco and Chicago fires.

The 1926 hurricane sent boats into the streets of downtown Miami and marked the beginning of the end of the 1920s land boom.

1927	Pan American Airways begins operations in Key West.
1928	Another hurricane ends the land boom, plunging Florida into a depression a year before the rest of the nation enters the Great Depression.
1930	Eastern Air Transport begins flights between Miami and New York.
1933	There is an unsuccessful attempt to assassinate President-elect Franklin Roosevelt in Miami.
1935	"Old Folks at Home" is named the state song.
1938	Marineland opens as a tourist attraction and movie studio.
1938	The Overseas Highway opens for cars, connecting Key West and the mainland.
1940	Naval Air Station Banana River opens, later becoming Cape Canaveral Space Center.
1941	Japan attacks Pearl Harbor, and Florida bases train hundreds of thousands of soldiers, sailors and airmen.
1945	World War II ends, and Florida's modern boom begins.
1947	Everglades National Park is dedicated.

Eastern Air Transport began service in Florida and in 1930 began service to New York.

One of the first major attractions in Florida was Marineland near St. Augustine. It was designed to be used as a tourist attraction and a setting for making movies.

1948	Florida State College for Women begins admitting men and becomes Florida State University.
1949	WTVJ becomes Florida's first television station.
1955	The legislature creates the state turnpike system.
1958	Explorer I, America's first earth satellite, is launched from Cape Canaveral.
1959	The Cuban Revolution overthrows the leader of Cuba, sending thousands of refugees to Florida.
1960	Florida becomes the tenth-largest state.
1961	Alan Shepard becomes the first American launched into space, taking off from Cape Canaveral Space Center.

1963   Following the death of President John Kennedy, Cape Canaveral and the Cape Canaveral Space Center are renamed for Kennedy. (In 1973, the town name of Cape Kennedy will be restored to Cape Canaveral.)

1964   There is rioting in St. Augustine as African American protestors attempt to integrate facilities.

1969   Apollo 11 astronauts blast off from Cape Kennedy on their way to the first moon landing.

1971   Walt Disney World opens in Orlando.

The opening of Walt Disney World in 1971 changed the economy of Florida forever.

The 1980 Mariel boatlift brought thousands of people from Cuba to Miami.

1980	The Mariel boatlift brings thousands of Cubans to Miami.
1982	EPCOT opens in Orlando.
1986	The space shuttle *Challenger* explodes shortly after takeoff from Cape Canaveral.
1990	Universal Studios Florida opens in Orlando.
1992	Hurricane Andrew strikes South Florida and causes extensive damage to Homestead.
2000	The presidential election between Al Gore and George W. Bush is decided by Florida. The election is too close to call, and the Florida electoral votes are in dispute. In the end, the Supreme Court awards the election to Bush.
2007	The booming Florida economy begins to crash as the nation's economy crumbles as a result of a housing bubble. It results in major state budget cuts and elimination of programs.
2010	The Space Shuttle program ends.
2014	Florida becomes the third-most populous state.

MAPS

All maps are courtesy of the Florida Department of Transportation.

MAP 1. SOUTHWEST FLORIDA

Counties
Charlotte, Collier, DeSoto, Glades,
Hardee, Hendry, Highlands, Lee,
Manatee, Okeechobee, Polk, Sarasota

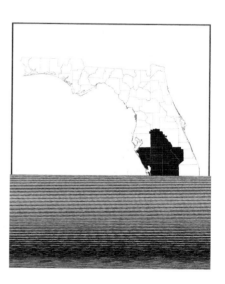

Attractions
• Bok Tower Gardens, Lake Wales
• Florida Southern College, Lakeland
• Ah-Tah-Thi-Ki Museum, Clewiston
• Cracker Trail Museum, Zolfo
  Springs
• De Soto National Memorial,
  Bradenton
• Edison and Ford Winter Estates,
  Fort Myers
• Gamble Plantation Historic State Park, Ellenton
• Manatee Village Historical Park, Bradenton
• Paynes Creek Historic State Park, Bowling Green
• The Ringling, Sarasota

MAP 2. NORTHEAST FLORIDA

Counties
Alachua, Baker, Bradford, Clay,
Columbia, Dixie, Duval, Gilchrist,
Hamilton, Lafayette, Levy, Madison,
Nassau, Putnam, St. Johns,
Suwannee, Taylor, Union

Attractions
- Cathedral of St. Augustine, St. Augustine
- Fort Mose Site, St. Augustine
- Hotel Ponce de Leon, St. Augustine
- St. Augustine Historical Society, St. Augustine
- *Maple Leaf*, Jacksonville
- Marjorie Kinnan Rawlings House and Farm Yard, Cross Creek
- St. Augustine Town Plan Historic District, St. Augustine
- Bronson-Mulholland House, Palatka
- Dow Museum of Historic Houses, St. Augustine
- Fort Carolina National Memorial, Jacksonville
- Fort Clinch State Park, Fernandina Beach
- Fort Matanzas National Monument, St. Augustine
- Fountain of Youth Archaeological Park, St. Augustine
- Historic Haile Homestead at Kanapaha Plantation, Gainesville
- Kingsley Plantation, Jacksonville
- Norman Studios Silent Film Museum, Jacksonville
- Spanish Military Hospital Museum, St. Augustine
- St. Augustine Lighthouse & Maritime Museum, St. Augustine
- Stephen Foster Folk Culture Center State Park, White Springs
- St. Augustine Historical Society Research Library, St. Augustine

MAP 3. NORTHWEST FLORIDA

Counties
Bay, Calhoun, Escambia, Franklin, Gadsden, Gulf, Holmes, Jackson, Jefferson, Leon, Liberty, Okaloosa, Santa Rosa, Wakulla, Walton, Washington

Attractions
- British Fort (Negro Fort), Sumatra
- Fort San Carlos de Barrancas, Pensacola
- Fort San Marcos de Apalache, St. Marks
- San Marcos de Apalache Historic State Park, St. Marks
- Fort Walton Mound, Fort Walton Beach
- *Governor Stone* Schooner, Panama City
- Pensacola Naval Air Station Historic District, Pensacola
- Plaza Ferdinand VII, Pensacola
- San Luis de Talimali, Tallahassee
- Arcadia Mill, Milton
- Florida State Capitol, Tallahassee
- Fort Barrancas, Pensacola
- Historic Plantation Village, Pensacola
- Museum of Florida History, Tallahassee
- T.T. Wentworth Jr. Museum, Pensacola
- Tallahassee Museum, Tallahassee
- Florida State Archives, Tallahassee
- The State Library of Florida, Tallahassee
- Florida State University, Tallahassee
- West Florida History Center, Pensacola
- Meek-Eaton Black Archives, Tallahassee

MAP 4. SOUTHEAST FLORIDA

Counties
Broward, Indian River, Martin, Palm
Beach, St. Lucie

Attractions
- Zora Neale Hurston House, Fort
  Pierce
- Mar-a-Lago, Palm Beach
- Whitehall, Palm Beach
- A.E. Backus Gallery & Museum,
  Fort Pierce
- Boca Express Train Museum, Boca
  Raton
- Richard and Pat Johnson Palm
  Beach County History Museum,
  West Palm Beach
- Society of the Four Arts, Palm Beach

MAP 5. CENTRAL FLORIDA

Counties
Brevard, Flagler, Lake, Marion,
Orange, Osceola, Seminole, Sumter,
Volusia

Attractions
- Mary McLeod Bethune Home,
  Daytona Beach
- Cape Canaveral Air Force Station,
  Cocoa
- Dade Battlefield, Bushnell
- Fort King, Ocala
- Ponce de Leon Inlet Light Station,
  Ponce Inlet
- The Research Studio, Maitland
- Windover Archaeological Site,
  Titusville

- Bulow Plantation Ruins Historic State Park, Flagler Beach
- Casa Feliz Historic Home Museum, Winter Park
- DeBary Hall Historic Site, DeBary
- Orange County Regional History Center, Orlando
- Florida Historical Society, Cocoa

MAP 6. SOUTH FLORIDA

Counties
Miami-Dade, Monroe

Attractions
- Marjory Stoneman Douglas House, Coconut Grove
- "Ferdinand Magellan," Miami
- University of Miami Special Collections, Miami
- Fort Zachary Taylor, Key West
- Freedom Tower, Miami
- Ernest Hemingway House, Key West
- USCGC *Ingham*, Key West
- Vizcaya, Miami
- Audubon House, Key West
- Deering Estate, Miami
- HistoryMiami, Miami
- Jewish Museum of Florida, Miami
- Mel Fisher Maritime Heritage Museum, Key West
- Truman White House, Key West
- University of Miami Special Collections, Miami

Map 7. West Central Florida

Counties
Citrus, Hernando, Hillsborough,
Pasco, Pinellas

Attractions
- Crystal River Site, Crystal River
- El Centro Español de Tampa,
  Tampa
- Safety Harbor Site, Safety Harbor
- Tampa Bay Hotel, Tampa
- Ybor City Historic District, Tampa
- Fort De Soto Park, Tierra Verde
- Fort Foster Historic Site,
  Thonotosassa
- University of South Florida Special
  Collections, Tampa

INDEX

L

M

ABOUT THE AUTHOR

James C. Clark is a senior lecturer in the History Department at the University of Central Florida, where he supervises the Florida Studies Program. He is one of Florida's leading historians, the author of ten books and the editor of a three-volume anthology of Florida writers. He has been honored by the Florida Historical Society, the Florida Society of Newspaper Editors and the Florida Magazine Association. He lives in Orlando, Florida.

Visit us at
www.historypress.com